JAMES JESS HANNON'S

FIVE MARKS

A CHRONICLE

ISBN: 1-4107-2976-1 (e-book)
ISBN: 1-4107-2977-X (Paperback)
ISBN: 1-4107-2978-8 (Dust Jacket)

This book is printed on acid free paper.

1stBooks - rev. 12/03/03

DEDICATION

To my wife, Virginia Christy Hannon

These few words carry the full measure of my gratitude. Your collaboration and contribution has been of such moment, had that avenue not been at hand the Chronicle, Five Marks, would yet be a box of handwritten pages.

James Jess Hannon

Photos of Oflag 64 prisoners on the road to Germany. I escaped during the evacuation and went east. These photos depict the weather that prevailed during my journey across Poland, Czechoslovakia, Hungary and Romania.

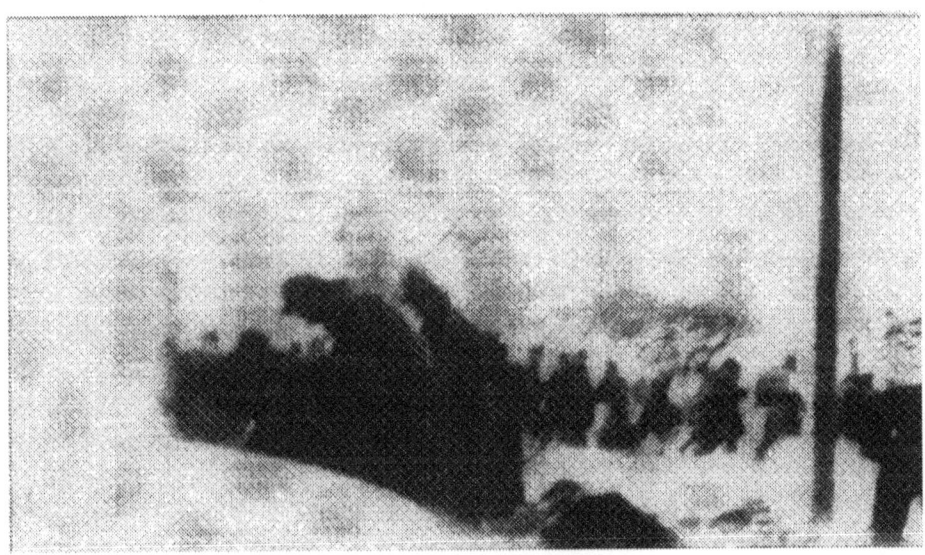

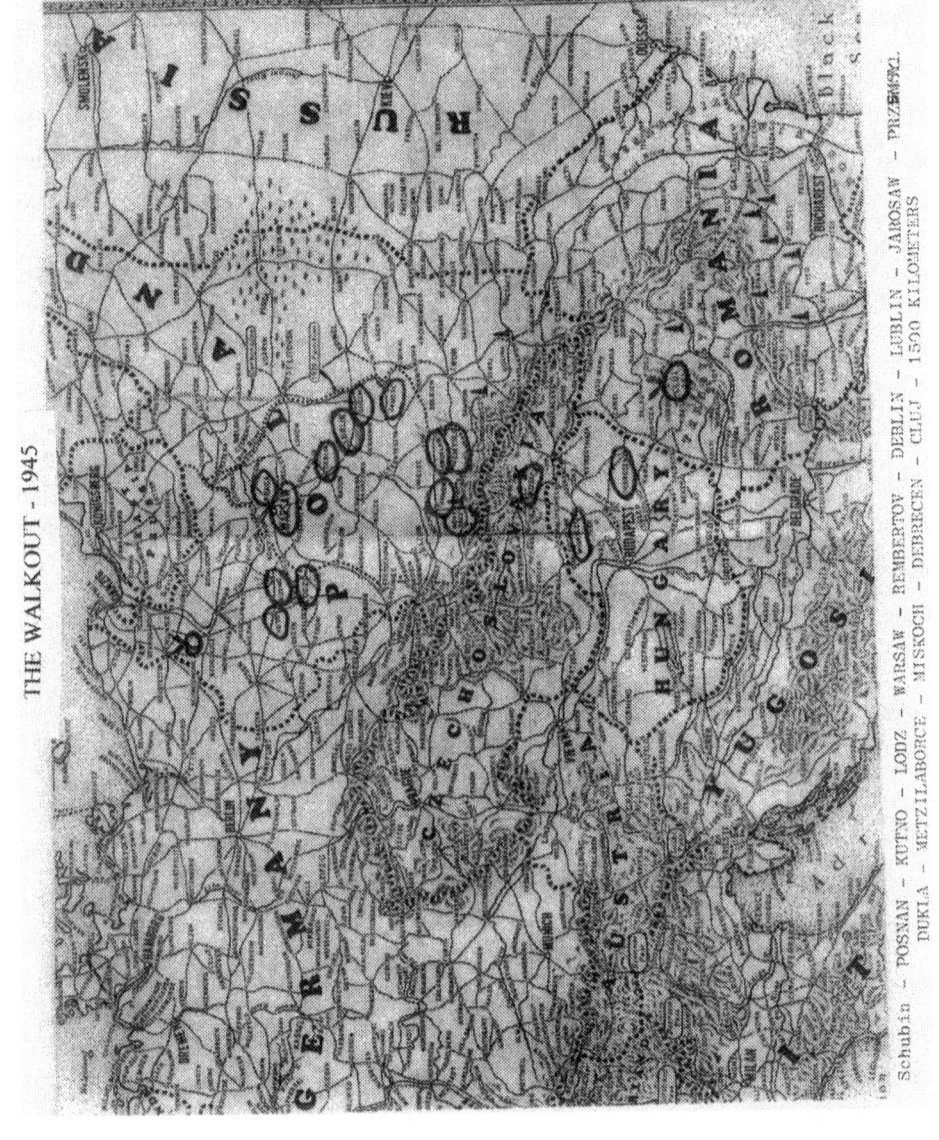

THE WALKOUT - 1945

Schubin - POSNAN - KUTNO - LODZ - WARSAW - REMBERTOV - DEBLIN - LUBLIN - JAROSAW - PRZEMYSL
PUKLA - METZILABORCE - MISKOCH - DEBRECEN - CLUJ - 1500 KILOMETERS

PROLOGUE

FIVE MARKS began, with urging from my beloved wife, shortly after I was honorably discharged from the U.S. Army. Many tides and versions of the German's barbaric crusade followed through the years. So it is, my final work may add a few revelations to that ghastly history not heretofore available.

Facts can be soft as picked cotton or granite hard. Still, the truth is indivisible or it is nothing.

Holocaust is a word I associated with fire – ultimate, consummate destruction.

German death camps, designed and constructed with precision by architects and engineers – Treblinki, Dachau, Maidonek and many other death camps defiled and poisoned the ground, the air, the dead and the living.

I was a prisoner in one, Dachau, Munich, Germany and as an escaped prisoner of war, absorbed the horror of Maidonek, Lublin, Poland.

An impressive inventory of first person chronicles written more skillfully than my work attested to the incredible conduct of the 'Master Race' and the fate of enemies of Hitler Aryan hordes; the final solution to the Jewish problem, how and why it happened, those outside the wire, the Russian soldier and much more.

Perhaps not until FIVE MARKS have so many near victims points of view been recorded while the war was reaching the long awaited apogee.

The behavior of the German soldier and civilian in the occupied countries challenges reason, their cruel excesses belonging to some long removed age in antiquity.

Above and beyond the Nazi nightmare the human spirit was revealed in both grandeur and horror.

I lived intimately with survivors at a time when passions had not cooled, the hell of genocide still in evidence, the conflict still raging. Count your blessings and remember, though we won the war it was too close for the survivors and too late for the victims.

CHAPTER I

A light, cool breeze sent dry leaves and paper scraps scurrying along the cobbled street.

Frank Fuller, Pete Grey and I had been brought together as only a hot war can, setting us apart, a feeling for each other unknown by those in the outside world.

We indulged our private fantasies without interruption except for an occasional remark provoked by a graceful, shy girl who averted her eyes as she passed our table.

Although the wine was red, cloudy and bitter, it built an easy, relaxed mood permitting thoughts of things far removed, underlying always the disquieting thought that we would soon catch up to the war.

A Jeep entered the square with a rush and squealing of tires. The drowsy peacefulness was shattered much as a galloping horse might send a farmyard into bedlam on a warm Sunday afternoon.

Skidding to a halt, the vehicle raised a curtain of dust that settled slowly as Captain Blythe stepped to the table, enveloped by a miniature whirlwind.

In a much too loud voice, he announced, "Lieutenant James Hannon!"

"Yes sir." I placed my elbows on the table, leaning forward expectantly.

"You're under arrest!"

As I lurched to my feet the table tipped, wine glasses and bottle shattering on the worn tile. Fuller and Grey remained seated.

"O.K., Captain, fill us in on the rest of the joke."

Ignoring Grey, the Captain stepped closer. "This is no joke, let's go, Lieutenant."

"We have a Jeep, we'll follow you, Captain."

Captain Blythe stepped back warily, his hand resting lightly on the holstered .45. "Are you coming, Lieutenant?"

I shrugged and spoke to the others, "Follow us..." I was no less surprised with my turn of fortune than were the men who knew me. I was, surely, an unlikely candidate for any charge warranting arrest.

Fuller was an inch shorter and twenty pounds heavier than I, a formidable physical specimen. On occasions he drank too much, but that was an indulgence most everyone shared.

Grey was a little removed from our closeness. We were platoon leaders in the same company, sharing the long voyage and all that followed.

The incredible ordeal began while I waited unbelieving as the vagaries were spelled out.

Major Watson studied the charges on his desk. He shook his massive head from side to side then leaned back and looked across the table. I met the stern look, matching it in intensity as the Major glanced around the room.

"At ease." He spoke quietly, almost kindly.

"Lieutenant, you should know the nature, the serious nature of these charges and the consequences to you – if they are true."

As he looked up slowly, the Major's face clouded. "Are they?"

The interval grew heavy and uncomfortable.

"What are the charges?" My words were barely audible.

The scene was unreal, incredible, not knowing the inherent danger in the threat waiting to assail me.

"You are charged and, according to this document, there is an abundance of substantiating evidence, Lieutenant, you are charged with three specific counts as follows: One, representing yourself as the Officer officially authorized to request information for this Headquarters from Base Headquarters; two, requesting classified information regarding future troop movements from this area, including destination of those movements."

Watson looked directly across the desk at me and, continuing to stare fixedly, went on. "And three, transmitting the information received to civilian persons, French and Arab in appearance, in public places off limits to military personnel."

The closing paragraph of the charges suggested that the civilian persons mentioned in count three could be construed as enemy agents.

"Well, Lieutenant?"

"Major Watson," I took a deep breath.

2

"Yes, Lieutenant?"

"I have never called anyone at Base Headquarters about anything. The charges are not true." I stopped, groping for stronger words. "I have no friends or acquaintances in Nemours among the Arabs or French."

"The calls were monitored, they all emanated from this area in your name and your serial number. You have been accused as the American Officer who met with local civilian persons and passed to them certain information. These local meetings, in every case, followed the telephone calls in a matter of hours."

"Major Watson, my assignment orders printed my name and serial number as it did the names and serial numbers of forty other officers and, like them, my name and serial number is stenciled on my Val Pak and Duffel bag. It is not classified information and is available to the public."

Major Watson struck a match, watched the flame thoughtfully. Just before it burned out he lit a cigarette and leaned back in his chair. "At 0400 tomorrow morning the regiment entrucks for Algiers to board ship." His voice trailed off. He smoked in silence for a moment. "You would be tried here."

I was devastated.

"I have an idea…" Watson picked up his telephone and turned the handle briskly. After mumbling something unintelligible, he shouted impatiently, "Major Watson, get me through to Colonel Reed, this is urgent."

Leaning across the desk, he offered a cigarette, I shook my head. Watson raised his eyebrows; he seemed preoccupied as he slowly placed the cigarettes back on his desk.

"Colonel Reed, this is Major Watson." Stopping abruptly, he smiled; the crackling voice on the other end of the line was audible to me. "Sorry, Colonel, didn't realize I was shouting."

He motioned to the two M.P. guards at the far end of the hut, held his hand over the mouthpiece. "It has to be this way, Lieutenant, at least for now."

A vast endless ceiling of stars overhead, clear and sparkling, imparted little light to the ground or the dark forms of the pyramidal tents.

3

I began the painful process of analyzing my predicament, knowing the charges were serious enough to destroy me. Who? Why? My impoverished childhood and unsettled lifestyle had left its mark. I had often felt that becoming a commissioned officer had been a mistake. As a boy I had been the object, countless times, of stinging references to the poverty that gave every slur the impact of physical assault, no matter that it was often shouted in fun or that there were other targets like me. For me it was personal, degrading and hard to understand.

I faced the incredible task of detaching myself from my predicament in an effort to find an answer. The charges were brazenly false, giving them unusual weight, leaving me groping for a logical explanation.

Colonel Reed, slight in stature, was an impressive and commanding figure. Handsome and erect, he moved with quick strides to the long table and took his place. He was flanked on one side by a bored, slack-faced Major Smith and on the other by the mustached, burly Lieutenant Colonel Bovard.

Major Watson sat quietly at one end of the table, his face inscrutable, the loosely held cigarette sending a thin, straight column of smoke upward where it was absorbed in the dense mixture under the low ceiling.

There were other men in the room to my right and left, but my interest was concentrated and directed to the three officers across the table.

"Lieutenant Hannon." Colonel Reed's glance and voice were harsh, piercing.

I moved to attention, "Yes, sir." I noted that I was the only person in the room standing.

"At ease, Lieutenant." Colonel Reed paused while he straightened papers on the table in front of him.

"Are you aware of the charges made against you here and now?" His voice had softened noticeably.

I opened my mouth, and then paused deliberately, knowing my answers must not be hurried or careless.

"I request the charges be read to me, Colonel." I spoke easily, displaying more confidence than I felt.

Colonel Reed's parade ground voice rose to a pitch jerking everyone erect in his chair.

"You did not answer my question, Lieutenant." He leaned forward aggressively.

"I'm sorry, sir."

"Well, I'm waiting for your answer…"

The Colonel seemed to rise from his chair, his hands holding the edge of the table.

"Charges were read to me some hours ago by Major Watson…" I paused, "…I request that they be read again."

Colonel Bovard smiled tolerantly, glancing confidently around the room. He turned to Colonel Reed, his tone was unctuous, "Colonel, the hour is past midnight, we are all weary, you more so than anyone…"

"Don't concern yourself about me, what is it you have to say?" Reed spoke sharply without turning his head.

Bovard's smile was a thing he wore as a permanent fixture; his eyes were slits, cruel and murderous. "Colonel Reed, I've read these charges and know the source of this information. I can assure you and the other officers here that they are factual and authentic. I see no reason to waste the time of men who will be moving out a few hours from now." He waved his hand in my general direction and added, "This man can be confined and tried later."

Watson pushed his chair back, stood up, walked around the table and took a position beside me.

"Colonel Reed…" Watson waited respectfully; the Colonel nodded his head almost imperceptibly.

"Sir, I believe this matter needs to be settled now." He looked directly at Bovard and continued. "I did not realize until this moment that Lieutenant Hannon is in dire need of an immediate trial. I suggest the charges be read before there is any further discussion."

A look passed between them.

"Read the charges, Major."

I listened intently, purposely keeping my eyes on an almost obscure calendar on the wall above Major Smith's head. As Smith concluded, I unconsciously smiled, continuing to look at the calendar.

"Lieutenant Hannon…" With a visible effort, Reed restrained his impulse to shout. "…I am completely without a sense of humor,

5

but I am damned if I can see anything pleasurable in this situation. What is it you find amusing?" He ended the question crashing his fist on the table.

I noted Watson's perplexed expression before I turned back to face Colonel Reed.

"Sorry, Colonel, the calendar reminded me this is my birthday."

Reed's facial expression relaxed, he seemed to sit more easily, leaning back and folding his arms.

Bovard shouted, "Congratulations, may they all be as memorable as this one." He laughed, then lapsed into silence as Colonel Reed pierced him with an eloquent stare and turned to face me.

"Whenever you're ready, Lieutenant."

Taking a deep breath, I looked directly at Colonel Reed, my voice deliberately low pitched.

"Sir, the name and serial numbers are mine. I have never represented myself to be anything but what I am, nor have I ever called anyone at Base Headquarters. I have no friends over here other than the officers and men who know me.

Looking deliberately at Bovard, I continued, "Anyone who states that he knows these charges to be true is mistaken. Someone may have used my name and serial number, I know nothing about that. The men who know me will leave here in a few hours, I am asking that you permit me to leave with the regiment and be tried by those who know me."

I felt a strong hand on my back. Major Watson spoke, "Colonel Reed, may I suggest we excuse Lieutenant Hannon momentarily."

"I don't think we can do that, Major. I have some questions and I'm sure others here have questions."

The Colonel was noticeably irritated as he turned over a sheet of paper. "Please sit down, Major."

I remained standing in the face of vicious tirades and accusations from Bovard, giving direct answers to Colonel Reed. Afterward, I knew that the man who seemed most determined to hurt me had turned the tide in my favor.

Bovard, enraged with my composure, leaned far over the table, spreading his hairy hands on the scattered papers.

"Lieutenant, you're lying. I give you my word, you are going to be tried wherever you are serving as soon as I can properly prepare charges." He turned dramatically to the Colonel, "Colonel, if there is any doubt, there is no doubt."

Carried away with the savage attack, the Colonel appeared deaf to Colonel Reed's shouted commands. Finally, he sat down heavily. "Lieutenant, I find the charges unsubstantiated. Therefore, I am releasing you from custody. You may proceed with your regiment. A copy of this hearing and findings will be inserted in your file. This inquiry is closed."

A cold, strong wind off the Mediterranean was in keeping with my mood. When I turned into the company street, Grey fell in beside me. "How did it go?"

"Charges were dropped."

Sixteen hours later we boarded a huge transport in heavy fog and before first light the throbbing engines pushed us out of Algiers Harbor.

CHAPTER II

In the early morning the city shoreline loomed deceptively peaceful. The scene defied the presence of the raging conflict sending its echoing rumbles over the gently rolling sea.

I stood transfixed as the pounding throbs propelled the vessel through the straits separating Capri from the mainland, sobered by the nearness of hot war.

Truck transport, long lines of identical vehicles, motors running awaited them. Naples Harbor revealed the shocking ugliness of total war.

Ships of immense tonnage had been blasted into piles of twisted scrap iron, on their keels, on their sides and on their bottoms, some out of water, blown onto the bayside shoreline and some were submerged beneath the still depths of the Bay of Naples.

I absorbed the impressive evidence of America's remarkable ability to get the job done, later learning the destruction in the harbor and adjacent shoreline had occurred during one U.S. Air Force daylight raid three months previous.

Loading docks and access roads had been constructed over and on the broken hulls. No time had been wasted attempting to clear the wreckage in the harbor critical to demands and needs of the 5th and 8th Armies.

It was early December; the weather was clear with a noticeable chill in the air. Absence of confusion was impressive; orders had meaning and those receiving them moved to carry them out.

We formed ranks, answered roll call and boarded the truck transport. From my position near the tailgate I could see enormous piles of supplies and massed ordinance. It appeared American troops were the sole occupants of the area.

Replacements were transferred for the most part to the 82nd Airborne Division as well as to various 5th Army Command Units. Three Officers and a platoon of troops were assigned to the 509th

Battalion for security duty at Capoduchino Airport on the outskirts of Naples. I was one of the three Officers.

It was soft duty; our presence put an end to looting. Battalion Headquarters located in a two-story schoolhouse in a working class suburb occasionally assigned me other duty.

It was there I experienced an incident still vivid in memory. As I exited the main entrance a sharp explosion followed by smoke and screams occurred across the street. Men in the motor pool and workshop joined me at the site.

Little ones, barely school age, had found a 60 mm mortar bomb, carried it to a road between houses and dropped it. We were sorting them out when the Battalion's Medical Corp arrived.

The devastated mother's and other family member's pathetic wailing and interference made our rescue efforts almost impossible. Major Kelly, Chief Medical Officer of our unit, ordered those he declared dead carried across the street to an open area in front of our Headquarters.

There were six, all of a pitiful size; their clothing was torn, and ugly wounds were visible. Captain Cosimo, Battalion Chaplin, gave the last rites and then the women went to their knees, caressing and kissing their dead little ones.

* * *

We crossed the harbor wreckage on metal sheets similar to temporary Air Force runways, filed into the cavernous hold of the LST, dropped our gear and sat down or stretched out in place until we heard and felt the ship moving; we were underway.

"How far Lieutenant?"

"I overheard an LST Officer on deck saying they were scheduled to drop the ramp at 0630, cruising speed 10 knots, offshore 10 – 12 miles, sea's calm. Measure it in time, they'll drop the ramp at 0630."

"Christ, that's all night."

"Go to sleep."

"Fat chance."

It was a long night and a longer day. Landing cost us a few hits, one fatal, then the move toward the hills, the start of the Apennines, the perimeter of the beachhead was an arc reaching inland 12

9

kilometers under long range German artillery and air attack. Mid-morning we saw a 10,000-ton U.S. freighter at anchor two miles offshore. Later, we learned it was carrying 500 troops and 8000 tons of ammunition. A Stuka dived out of the overcast and dropped his load. The freighter showed a wide flash, a black cloud and a rumbling explosion. When it cleared, the ship had vanished and so had the Stuka.

Full field packs and air attack alerts made the walk an all day exercise. At five in the afternoon the guide called a halt in an orchard.

"We stay here until dark; your dinner's cooking behind those trees – fill up, you'll like the chow, it'll be hard to find when you dig in."

He had that right — roast beef, potatoes, gravy and hot biscuits might be our last good meal for a while.

After dark we formed up and marched on a hard surface, then filed off the road and sat down or stretched out behind a house and outbuildings. Phosphorous shell bursts, U.S. variety, resembled Fourth of July fireworks. A burst in slow motion, or so it seemed, blossomed in colors floating to the ground. In a way that was impersonal, machine gun tracers crossed the front; we were not involved, at that moment we were spectators.

The Command Post, a white stucco villa, showed no sign of occupation; it was one among others on the road to Corona.

"Lieutenant Hannon reporting."

A door opened just enough for me to enter and move around the blanket to the side.

"Sit down, Lieutenant – coffee?"

"Thank you, sir."

Major Grace, his brown hair showing a sprinkling of gray, seemed tense and nervous. He sat on the far side of a common kitchen table; behind him, a wood stove filled the room with heat and smoke.

"You'll report to 'B' Company with Lieutenant Fuller, Lieutenant Grey to 'A' Company. Lieutenant Casper is 'B' Company Commander.

"You'll hear it enough, but I can't overemphasize, keep down in those foxholes from daylight to dark, manage to do everything, and I mean everything, at night; those foxholes are home. New men will become veterans fast, but, until you do, don't be misled when there's

10

a quiet spell. Sergeant Duncan will take you up. You'll have a hot breakfast at four thirty – glad you're here."

As I was passing several non-coms in the yard I overheard an exchange.

"How many?"

"Two, Private John R. Danby, Corporal Jedifer Remington."

I stopped in mid-stride and turned. "Did you say Corporal Jedifer Remington?"

"Yes sir, 1st Platoon, Company 'A'."

"Where is he?"

"Far end, next to supply."

The need had announced itself with a banging of drums and a blare of trumpets during his first training cycle.

Years of unadorned instruction in the practiced areas of book learning according to the views of those unloved, devoted servants of the Lord had literally hammered into me what now seemed a remarkable store of matter, enabling me to pass on to others knowledge available only in books or the storehouse of men's minds.

My special challenge, one Private Jedifer Remington, a name evoking pictures of the mythical, gallant southern Civil War officer portrayed in one of my favorite motion picture, 'Gone With The Wind'. The name and romantic image had been misleading; the tall, gangly recruit was topped off with sprouting, corn tassel hair; he was an authentic Arkansas hillbilly. His physical inadequacies were not the least of his problems attested to by his classification as Category 3, reading and writing skills borderline, plus such an extraordinary lack of physical coordination he was to become an object of frustration and scorn to his perspiring comrades who bitched and swore in outrage.

Jedifer's unpredictable blunders caused a portion of every close order drill to become a Laurel and Hardy disaster compelling veteran Sergeant Blake to clench his fists, look skyward and plead for mercy. He simply could not make his body or its parts move in unison with other bodies in the most basic of all military drills, the 'lock step'.

I placed him in the rear file where I could coach the bewildered Private and minimize the resulting chaos.

Jedifer was a product of Arkansas backcountry, light years removed from the America I had roamed. In the nineteen years of his life Jedifer had not spent one year in a schoolroom, his sporadic attendance terminated during his second year. Thereafter, formal school learning ceased.

Despite all of the unpromising evidence, during a span of four weeks as an enthusiastic attendant at my 'readin' and 'writin' clinic, he topped the class properly by writing his name, reading numbers on barracks doors and counting his place in formation.

The pace and ritual of accelerated military training was, to him, a confusing blur of events swallowing each other in a continuous process of shouted commands, all carried on at a pace that compounded his every blunder.

When the schedule of free time permitted, I taught him how to relax, keep his head up and count. In time, he began to grasp the science of coordinated body control and, eight weeks into the cycle mastered the 'lock step'.

His newly acquired skill triggered the first gleanings of self-confidence and a personal awareness of other assets. A remarkable change was occurring in this tall, blue-eyed boy. To the utter amazement of his detractors, he found his voice. With that and twenty additional pounds, his almost belligerent response to tormenters worked a small miracle; the heckling came to a halt.

I enjoyed a rare feeling of satisfaction. Without overdoing things, I continued to encourage and coach the emerging soldier until the training cycle was in the process of sharpening the acquired skills. And then, Jedifer Remington paid back, with interest, all of the patient hours I had invested in him.

The shooting was in the qualifying stage. Skill and proficiency would be a permanent item on the service record and provide a medal attesting to the category of the soldier's skill.

Jedifer's target shooting completed his meteoric ascendancy from clodhopper to first class infantry soldier. He out shot his squad, his platoon, his company and terminated the training cycle by posting the highest score ever recorded in his Battalion at Camp Williams.

On completion of the cycle he had been shipped with four hundred battalion graduates to an embarkation center destined as infantry replacements for the Mediterranean Theater of Operations. A little sadly, I wished his platoon good luck and walked to my quarters absorbed in the harsh reality of their purpose.

"This is what it's all about, Lieutenant." Sergeant Blake's words brought me out of my reverie.

"Of course – still – how ready are they?"

"Thirteen weeks ready."

The Sergeant's terse response summed up the true state of America's readiness for the biggest war in history.

I groped through the blankets and stood inside the Aid Station for a moment as my eyes adjusted to the unshaded light. A strong draft of warm air and potent mixture of odors assailed me. Three field hospital beds along one wall were occupied.

"What can I do for you?"

A short, too heavy Captain walked towards me craning his neck.

"Lieutenant Hannon, which one is Corporal Remington?"

"Over there, under the tarp."

We exchanged looks.

"I'd like to see him."

"Help yourself."

The Captain turned away and busied himself at a table loaded with various sized bottles.

A pair of scuffed combat boots poked out from under the covering tarp. I stepped to the far end, crouched, then slowly pulled back the tarp and froze in place.

Matted, corn silk hair askew, sky blue eyes wide open, a bloody, dried froth around his mouth, Jedifer Remington's enduring expression marked the instant of his confrontation with the force that struck him down, a look reborn with each appalling intrusion that had slammed in succession into his awakening conscience. His marble skin had a polished sheen reflecting the barely discernible golden stubble covering his lower face matching the strands of hair spread across his forehead.

Perhaps his expression came with a new discovery as foreign to his pristine nature as the affronts occasioned by an abrasive world never known in his early years. His countenance suggested a vision so consuming he was stunned. I truly hoped Jedifer Remington had found paradise.

Dropping to my knees, I enacted a ritual from days long gone. Quietly, in that barren corner, I gave an invocation asking the Holy

Father to receive the soul of Corporal Jedifer Remington and then I stood up, astonished by my act.

The simple ceremony caused a rare feeling of emotion as I covered the remarkably childlike face. Death had stripped away the emerging man lines, not in place long enough to be permanent.

I stood up slowly. Suddenly, all the fatigue that had been gathering caused me to drop my head as I turned away. Captain Burns blocked my way.

"Price of real estate's pretty high over here."

I looked hard at the grinning Captain. "For some."

"Are you a Chaplain?" The abrasive voice matched his rude manner.

I shook my head and moved to the exit.

"Who the hell are you?"

I turned away and answered, "A friend."

The attack was a disaster; losses were heavy. In retrospect, I was a borderline loser, not critical; it was more a feeling that we had some catching up to do.

Replacements brought us a trade-off, but left us short in numbers. Fortunately, we had time and the enemy seemed content to stay on the defensive. So it was, we went through the holiday season holding in place.

CHAPTER III

I leaned against the back wall of the foxhole watching the machine gun tracers criss-crossing the front as phosphorous shell bursts blossomed among the German positions.

Lieutenant Fuller and Sergeant Duncan crouched close.

"You know the drill, our big stuff will open at a four o'clock; at five, green flares, we move out when the barrage lifts."

I turned and faced them. "It might work, Sergeant."

"We can hope, it'll be a nasty son-of-a-bitch if we get stalled on that slope."

Low on the eastern horizon a rapid, flaring light showed as the heavy rumbling mixed with swishing sounds overhead and thunderous explosions on higher ground to our front. Green flares moved us out in good order until we reached the weather-scarred slope.

Curtains of dust, mortar bursts and small arms fire drove us to the ground. I signaled until the platoon found concealment from small arms fire. We were still vulnerable to the big stuff.

Mortar bomb fragments, rock particles, small arm projectiles, direct hits and ricochets punished the company without pause. Communication with adjoining units became impossible. I was still in radio contact with battalion headquarters issuing a continuous flow of commands and futile requests for information.

"State your casualties…estimate your ETA on objective…"

At one o'clock the mortar and small arms fire increased. Efforts to advance the platoon or hold it together dissolved in that inescapable trap. Control vanished when the continuous fire of heavy weapons drowned out attempts to contact men who were a short few feet away.

Watching a soldier stand up, drop his rifle and begin walking to the rear, I threw a rock and shouted between the crashing explosions, "Get down – hit the ground…"

Throwing his hands in the air, the soldier spun full circle and sprawled face down.

I shouted, "Don't move, stay where you are..." A volley of exploding mortars drowned my words.

A close burst threw up a covering cloud of dust and smoke as I lunged, half-erect, to my left behind a hard shelf breaking out from the slope. Pressing down into the rough dirt clutching my rifle, my left hand touched something warm and sticky; a small whimpering voice repeated over and over, "Help me, help me...."

Turning my head, I froze for a moment then screamed, "Goddam – goddam them!"

I was looking at a boy soldier. I pulled his hand from his guts. Below the navel there was nothing, yet he lived or seemed to, crying, unmoving, eyes wide open, staring heavenward.

"Help me..."

Pushing the muzzle of my rifle close behind the boy's ear, I froze, then rolled to the shelter of an upthrust and looked at the wound on the inside of my left knee with no recollection of pain or impact. A dressing stopped the bleeding.

It came to be the most haunting day I would ever know, removed from the action as intermittent lulls and volleys pinpointed precise areas.

I searched for a shelter, found it and scanned the high ground, heard the whistle of a descending bomb, the heavy thud as it burst behind me and felt a smashing breath-taking blow beneath my shoulder that put me face down motionless.

Much later I became aware of distant noises, artillery thuds and automatic fire. Total darkness caused a moment of near panic until I saw flashes on the valley floor, stars overhead and said a small prayer looking at Garibaldi Cemetery outlines.

CHAPTER IV

Each day there was an hour I had come to dread, a time that almost dragged me under. It was the small hours before first light, impossible then to delude myself or take any comfort from the vagary of hope. It was my 'moment of truth' when time seemed frozen in place. The insignificance of my role, the futility of my efforts, the brevity of my journey and, finally, the certainty of my destruction were like hammer blows overwhelming more rational views. It was not just the constant threat as much as the feeling that I had been abandoned. The receding past seemed out of reach and the dreams on hold would never be.

I whispered solemnly the prayer I had offered each bedtime of my childhood, "Our father, who art in heaven..." the words yielded a dwindling comfort, softening the ugliness of the fate that was becoming fixed. It was an image reflecting so much of the dark underside of man's nature the one in view became clouded and obscure. My sense of solitude caused a wave of terrible loneliness to come down with such force my shoulders slumped and my head sank lower into the folds of the blanket, a shield providing an imagined security holding out ugly truth.

I remembered reading that sick people were more likely to die in the early morning hours. I pulled the blanket closer as the cold and depression worsened.

The curving arc of distant machine gun tracers was followed by the muted sounds of firing bringing thoughts about a lucky hit that could be a ticket home or a not so lucky hit similar to the one that dismembered Lieutenant Kraus.

One day it would end, word would come down to both sides. Germans and G.I.'s would meet out there at the bottom of the slope and, for sure, someone in the last minute or the last second would step on a mine.

There were fuzzy edges and gray areas. Some old canards had worn thin — 'a righteous cause', the 'good guys' and 'the bad guys', 'God's on our side'; it had come down to survival with the growing conviction there was little I could do to bring it off.

I thought about those back home, doing their jobs like people everywhere, all moving towards something no one could define beyond the vagaries of righteous references to God and country as though they were synonymous terms, take from it what you will.

A barely discernible change in the inky blackness of the eastern sky and the fluttering whistle of an incoming howitzer ended my reverie, an ear-splitting explosion, an intense barrage, the precursor to an infantry assault.

I spun around, kicked the sleeping private awake, raised myself above the rear side of the trench and shouted, "Mortar – mortar!"

I was about to repeat the command when the bright flash burst overhead. I moved into position.

Fifty yards out, an irregular line hugged the ground contrasting with the yellow grain stubble like figures on a movie screen.

Near the center of the line, two Germans crouched motionless over a foxhole that had sheltered the occupants. Before I squeezed off the first round, both men plunged to the ground, sprawling motionless beside their target.

Germans rolled and twisted, searching out depressions or crawling into shallow furrows, frantically trying to return the fire. Finally, they broke for the shelter of the cemetery leaving the field marked with the victims of their assault.

As the light faded, I propelled myself out of my foxhole and dropped into the next; a huddled form tripped me. Reaching out, my fingers moved gently upward, feeling the lips, the nose and the soft sunken eyes; my throat tightened as I made a warm, sticky contact, blood, clingy and sticky, worked in between my fingers. A face became fixed in my memory; with a slender hand covering his eyes, tears were cutting furrows in the brown dirt on his cheeks.

A night a week past, my patrol had circled the walled cemetery several hundred yards beyond the base of the slope and stopped near battered marble statuary to let the squad close up.

We returned through the company area and continued on to report and rest for the day at headquarters occupying a two-story farmhouse with the usual outbuildings.

We ate the hot breakfast in weary silence, then sat out long moments sipping steaming coffee and smoking chain fashion until I spoke without raising my eyes from my cup. "You're off duty until four o'clock, have fun."

I stepped outside, studied the outbuildings and walked behind the nearest one, sat down on a patch of straw, removed my helmet and pistol belt and leaned back against the barn wall. Loosening my clothing, I stretched my arms, settling into a half-sitting, half-lying position. The feeling was one of uncommon comfort, the mid-morning sun warming my muscles and stiff, aching joints. Through half-closed eyes, I gazed casually across the flat, orderly landscape sloping gently downward away from the barn to a distant line of trees.

Morning haze obliterated the small details. Here and there clusters of white houses, outbuildings and gray road patterns gave no sign of the violence that had passed over and rumbled at the foot of a hill mass five kilometers to the north.

"Lieutenant..."

Lindsey was standing two paces away, shuffling his feet nervously, and easing his tall, angular frame back against the barn. Soiled jacket and trousers, grubby hands and unshaven, tired face displayed the outward image of the foot soldier. The result was uniformity, sameness, and the language of war, as casually acquired as the other parts.

With Lindsey it was different. He might use the same words, but they didn't work, and the shabby, soiled garments didn't seem right. The total effect was ludicrous; he tried to be like the others, how he tried – it never worked.

I told him to sit down.

"Lieutenant..." His manner was awkward, hesitant, marked by a note of urgency.

"What's on your mind?"

"My back, Lieutenant, I wrenched my back while we were unloading ammo after breakfast."

I stood, straightened my jacket, brushed the dust from my pants and then buckled on my pistol belt. As I reached for my helmet, Lindsey moved closer.

"Could you speak to the Colonel, Lieutenant? I can type..." His voice was rising. "I've talked to the battalion clerk, they need help."

"So do we, Lindsey." I stepped away from the wall.

Lindsey seized my arm. "I can't go back, Lieutenant! Maybe the others don't feel it, I don't care what anyone thinks — I can't go back!"

He paused for a moment and tried to regain his composure. "I've done my share, Lieutenant, I've done my share – if you send me out there again, it's the end for me!" He stopped abruptly, placing his hands over his eyes.

"We've all felt the same way, Lindsey, try not to think about it." Then, because I had no adequate answer, I turned away.

How little it would have mattered, the disturbing thought of some men compelled to deliver all of themselves. In astonishment I realized I had become a part of the madness.

Much later, crouching by the still warm body, I was up tight against a wall in the impenetrable darkness. "Jesus Christ, what's to become of us?"

I began the process of thinking about things at hand. Feeling around for a blanket, I straightened the body and, as though trying to keep out the clammy cold, carefully covered Lindsey. I started to recite a prayer and stopped abruptly. My escaping breath could have been a sigh of fatigue or a curse or a combination of both as I turned and climbed out of the foxhole.

CHAPTER V

How would it come? Don't think about it was the sage advice our Chaplain, Captain (Father) Doyle, gave us. Well meant but meaningless; what else could he say? Something clean and quick, from this world to the next without time to think about it.

Lieutenant Paye at first light crawled out of his hole and started for the streambed where he jogged in place, did push-ups and other physical routines; he was a fighter, a pugilist.

It was sudden death. The German 88 was aimed like a rifle and hit before you could hear the sharp crack when it left the barrel. Paye disappeared as he approached the streambed; all they found was a scalp covered with curly black hair.

Private Duncan looked like he was sleeping; a clean piece of steel protruded from both sides of his head above the ears.

Glancing at the Corporal huddled on a pad in the trench, I decided to let him sleep a while longer.

Lieutenant Ross, an expert at disarming land mines. (Who would ever volunteer to disarm mines?) He worked sitting down with the mine in his lap. Something went amiss that day, the mine exploded taking both legs, both arms, and his eyes – he lived.

Sometimes it was clean. Sergeant Perkins, name may be wrong, lying prone raised his head to watch a column of Wermacht approaching the front; he never moved, remained there until they pulled him back; the sharp shooter put the bullet right between the Sergeant's eyes, a clean shot.

Two Lieutenants raced for the foxhole when the first round hit close to the line; they literally dove into the shelter. An 88 round hit on the slope, plowed through the soil and found them; identification was, fortunately, confirmed by their 'dog tags.

Occasionally, I counted those who were no longer with us; those I knew in training, jump school, on the ship crossing the South Atlantic, those who were assigned to the 82nd Division. We heard by rumor that the count was on a par with ours. Add to it those unknown to me – the young soldier in two pieces crying out for help.

* * *

Removing my equipment, I stretched and began preparing my solitary luxury, scalding hot coffee. With great care I adjusted the blanket, checking and re-checking every fold and corner to be certain no pinhole of light would escape. Finally, I began the ritual, boiling the water longer than necessary, slowly pouring and stirring the concentrate then sipped and smoked, drained the cup, pinched out the cigarette, wrapped the blanket around my shoulders and moved to the aperture. The night air was cold, damp cold; an unusual silence in the darkness was ominous.

Gazing across the dark, shadowy slope, occasional tracers and shell bursts flared and died on the far side of the cemetery; it was an interval for reflection or wondering.

The brief moments of tense action, the long, interminable lonely nights, I awaited pre-dawn hours with an unnatural dread. My escape was the winding trail back into the world of good things I had enjoyed, moments I would never forget.

"Lieutenant Jim Hannon…" The first time I was addressed that way the air seemed charged, the feeling electric. The ceremony was short and deeply moving. A surging pride engulfed me when it struck home – an officer in the Army of the United States.

"The honor and privilege to be one of the leaders in the forward ranks in the noble struggle that looms ahead, the struggle to preserve democracy." The Colonel's words, however trite they might sound under different circumstances, penetrated. My pride at that moment was a revelation, something strange and humbling came alive.

I saw the phosphorus bursts on the far slope and heard the scattered rattle of distant machine guns persistently and stubbornly agitating for a flare up, but my mind was replaying bits and pieces of the past.

Through an uncertain childhood and the tumultuous years in abrasive arenas of the commercial world, I had forged a singular way of life, became a private person, conditioned to conceal uncertainties and fears. I knew fear having been exposed more than most to forces capable of doing me great harm.

The dead, violated and profaned in countless ways caused me to turn away. Without life the body became an object, 'they're out of it', or 'that's not him'.

The occasion when I delivered the personal effects of several dead officers to the shipping warehouse in Naples was brought to mind. Laid out in long lines on the dock floor in separate piles were musette bags, valpacks and footlockers. Musette bags and valpacks were flat — empty. I lifted a few footlockers – they revealed the same lightness.

A Captain in charge was candid. "That's right, Lieutenant, those that haven't been robbed by the time we get 'em are rare. What the hell, if they don't steal the stuff here, what do you think those States side buzzards will do?"

A trip to Battalion Headquarters reporting the last few day's events to the Adjutant was routine. Lunch was a feast by front line standards. I lingered at the table indulging until I was satiated. In need of fresh air, I walked outside toward a tree line.

They were laid out behind the barn. I went down the line raising the shelter half covers to see who had bought it; some faces stirred vague memories.

Better times flooded my mind of Naples, Sorrento, candlelight, music and Captain Don Schmidt. I knelt a long time staring at the face that had been as handsome as a screen idol.

Leaning against the barn wall I stared across the quiet land and saw myself on a litter, bloody, lifeless, dog tags pinned to my jacket; all I had learned and felt would go in the ground with me.

The sun had vanished, twilight shadows erasing tree lines and clusters of buildings. I turned and walked towards the Jeep.

"Any time, Sergeant."

"Not dark enough, Lieutenant, have a cup of coffee."

Twenty minutes later, we turned out of the yard and headed towards the rumbling, flaring line visible across the horizon. As we approached the point of no return the Jeep stopped.

"Far as I go, Lieutenant."

Sergeant Wright watched him striding toward the inferno, a silhouette, diminishing until he vanished in the void.

"They go back, just like that, will anyone ever know why?"

CHAPTER VI

Sergeant Tracy laid his rifle with their weapons at the back of the shelter cut into the stream bank. The original occupants had placed timbers overhead and piled on several feet of packed mud.

"Still raining?" I was making conversation; the steady sound of rain could be heard in the stream.

"No change."

"I'll visit the troops, it's ten after five, hold the fort."

The ground was slick as grease, with a steady rain. I raised a shelter half and spoke to the soldier. "Be getting light in an hour or so, maybe, if they hit us take the target in front of you. Do what you have to do now."

I moved down the line passing on what I could, knowing morale, that's what they call fear, was gnawing away along with the miserable conditions staying alive in a hole in the ground. The Lieutenant I relieved was in a hurry as though he had a train to catch.

"Dig in deep, Lieutenant, tell them to stay in those stinking holes – see you later…"

They were gone before we were in place. I had a gut feeling we were in deep trouble as a machine gun sent tracers too low into our line. I made my way into our C.P., laid my weapon on the pile, took off my pistol belt and laid down beside Tracy.

"How they doin'?"

"They 'ain't' doin', Sergeant."

I glanced at my watch – ten minutes before six – then it happened – cracking explosions, screaming, shell and rock fragments, whistling mortar bombs, dirt pouring down from overhead, booming artillery guns, ground moving, a hurricane of noise. It went on and on, still building, stretching seconds into minutes. The overhead timbers flew, letting an avalanche of mud bury us. Fighting and shouting, I rolled on my hands and knees as Tracy screamed, "Get out – get out".

We scrambled to our feet as the barrage moved on. Germans were swarming up the hill through the minefield; a quick glance showed them already beyond our line. Weaponless, we ran for the shelter of the brush lining the stream's banks and stopped in water up to our hips. German shouts and automatic fire drove us farther into the shelter of the bushes. I landed beside a Corporal with a hole in his chest, eyes and mouth open, blood gushing out; I closed his eyes.

"Raus – Raus."

Four of the Germans on the bank had us dead cold in their sights. Tracy, in the water, held up his hands; I stood up and raised my hands.

Responding to the shouted 'Raus', we climbed up the bank and stopped facing a grinning Corporal with a dirty bandage around his neck and his right hand outstretched, palm up.

I gave him my wallet; Tracy did the same. Money in hand, the Corporal spoke to the others then said, "Cigarette". We obliged, then I glanced to the slope in front of our positions; Germans were sprawled there, some in the minefield. Other Company 'B' troops were sitting at the bottom of the field; guards were smoking. Our defensive line had been wiped out. In a state of shock, Tracy and I carried a young, badly injured enemy on a blanket to the Aid Station at the bottom of the rise.

CHAPTER VII

A strong, sour odor caused me to catch my breath. The cellar had been dug out in the form of a catacomb. One long corridor ran straight through and opened into a small circular room with a single light bulb hanging from the ceiling.

Directly under the light an operating table had been placed and a perspiring, middle-aged German wearing a blood stained, once white smock was attending a casualty. He gave no sign he was aware of the prisoners and the casualty on the litter. In time a motion with his hand signaled attendants who removed the patient from the table. Casting a swift glance toward Tracy and I, he pointed to the table. We placed the soldier as directed and stepped back. The Doctor probed, wiped his hands on his smock and turned facing me. Resignation, frustration and numbing fatigue left no room to register emotion. He placed his hand on the table and shook his head. We carried the litter into the main corridor and followed the guard until he stopped and pointed to a vacant spot in the long line of casualties, their moans and pleadings filling the corridor.

As we started toward the entrance feeling an urgent need for fresh air, the guard suddenly snapped to attention as a smallish Officer walked down the ramp. Neat and dapper, wearing a field-green uniform and green cape fastened at the neck, he stopped and casually ordered us in English.

"Step outside, join your comrades."

Greetings were brief and casual with the American prisoners close to the house. Lieutenant Lewis, lying full length with his hands folded across his stomach, opened his eyes and turned his head. I had met him several times at briefings.

" 'B' Company, they sent me up just before the attack with a message, full alert, anticipate strong enemy assault."

"They had that right."

"Something nicked me in the belly."

I knelt and pulled the clenched hands away as Lieutenant Lewis protested. There wasn't much blood; I uncovered the wound and caught my breath, his lower abdomen had been slit open, and intestines were bursting through an ugly tearing wound. I stood up and walked back to the entrance where the Officer was conversing with the guard.

"One of my comrades is badly wounded."

It seemed like a futile request considering the number of German wounded in the basement. To my surprise, the Officer walked into the cellar and returned with two guards.

"They will go with you. We do not have much as you can see."

Placing Lewis on the litter, we carried him down the corridor to the table under the light. The Doctor peered intently at the wound, poked with his fingers and grunted to himself then turned and repeated the impersonal shake of the head. I opened my mouth to protest, but the Doctor had already spoken to the bearers who stepped quickly to the table.

Lewis stared at the Doctor as he was carried away. After he was placed at the end of the line, I sat down beside him at a loss for words.

"I didn't think it would happen to me."

I wanted to convince him the Doctor had made a mistake, it didn't come out that way.

"Damn it, if our people had you…"

"But they don't – it could be worse, there's no pain."

"How about a cigarette?"

"No thanks." He shut his eyes and turned to the wall.

I sat quietly smoking, occasionally glancing toward Lewis until a loud, grating voice brought me up.

Other prisoners were getting to their feet as I joined the group. A Corporal searched each man, placing anything of value in a pile at his feet. When he found photographs of women he viewed them from different angles then returned the photos with a smirk and a comment to the other guards that drew a laugh

Search completed, we were herded into the cellar, assigned a litter and ordered outside. Tracy and I stayed close together, picked up a litter and moved out. At the top of the ramp we joined a line of other prisoners carrying litters as the procession slowly began its journey toward the high ground and a white city in the green hills above the beachhead

It was the beginning of the most grueling physical ordeal I would ever know. No stranger to physical challenges, I would push the limits of my endurance before the sun set.

Each step was an effort defying all efforts to maintain any rhythm between the bearers. We stumbled, tripped and cursed the insanity of the guards who denied us the dry shoulders, insuring the prolonged torture of those on the litters.

The stinking bog occasionally revealed bloated or flattened corpses being ground into the gluey mixture along with other assorted debris of war.

A clear blue sky added no impediment to the blazing fireball high above the eastern hills sucking up steamy wisps from the ribbon of festering muck.

To our right, the walking wounded moved apace, glancing occasionally at a line of replacements moving toward the front who stared at the funereal parade crawling away from the rumbling front, shouting unintelligible remarks to the retreating, used-up rejects.

Our burden was pumping out blood awash on the litter and spilling over when we stumbled. Bearers in front and behind fell to their knees at ever increasing intervals making a mockery of our efforts.

We waited for the column to start up, offered no respite from the misery of that senseless march. The indifference of the guards added to the ordeal. Walking on dry paths beside the road, they responded with shouts and threats that were lost on the disintegrating prisoners.

Time stood still as sounds from the front dwindled into mid-day doldrums. We passed in and out of mental blackouts that was, in a way, a blessing permitting the only relief available. When the sun was directly overhead, we were ordered off the road and directed into a vineyard bordering an olive orchard.

We stood dumb and faint, akin to beasts of burden, until a slender blond Captain motioned us to put the litters down. His voice and manner coupled with his blond hair and clean features made him an intruder in that senseless ordeal.

The Captain knelt beside us. He unwound the bloody bandage, dressing the wounds, and gently wrapped the slippery, elastic binding.

29

There was a physical similarity between him and the semi-conscious man on the litter whose wounds made the Captain's efforts little more than a gesture.

He moved from one to another, totally dedicated to the plight of the casualties, a futile effort in the eyes of his silent audience. I wondered if this service might have kept him from becoming a victim of the monstrous tragedy.

Turning from one mangled wreck, his eyes locked with mine for an instant, his expression strangely close to anger, then he mumbled something in German, flipped a quick hand wave or salute and walked away as the jarring scream of the Corporal drove us to our feet, out of the orchard, past the dry footpath and into the dreaded bog where the stench and impediments had worsened.

The prisoner ahead of me collapsed into the morass, then both bearers sprawled full length. When they stood and picked up the litter they were driven hard to close the gap.

Something happened that took me out of that hellish place, still present physically, yet, in some strange limbo, the sharp edges dull and blurred. Fatigue, pain and heat were all lumped together; somehow my body had adjusted letting me accept and endure whatever was to come.

Shouts and noises of the plodding column joined together. I looked up for a moment as a fighter plane roared toward us, its wings scant feet above the bordering orchards. The pilot's goggles flashed as he turned his head.

I saw the column of replacements and guards dive into the ditch, seemingly unaware of the column's exposure, moving without thought or purpose.

My mental state approached hallucination; I saw Velletri just above the orchard and was unable to relate it to my ordeal.

Artillerymen gathered close to the road watching the procession. They neither shouted nor threatened; some were whittling idly on sticks or smoking, mildly curious, nothing else. All of them seemed to have the attitude of bored spectators watching an all too familiar pageant.

The trickle of blood made my grip uncertain, I called to the aid men and pointed. We were shouted off the road under the withering glance of the non-com. I took advantage of the halt, sitting down slowly and stretching out on my back. For the moment, nothing else mattered. The sensation was exquisite, pain and fatigue seemed to be flowing out of my body as I watched the aid man trying to adjust the tourniquets while the soldier on the litter groaned and babbled. When he released the rubber binding, the blood poured over his hands and the bandages became so slippery he called one of the guards to help him.

Every device I could muster was employed in order to be less aware of my fading strength. For a time, I concentrated on the limping, staggering line of German wounded; some had fashioned crutches from olive trees. I thought if the column had been turned so it headed back toward the front, in all likelihood, every man would have blindly followed.

The sun seemed closer, hanging overhead, bearing down relentlessly; there seemed to be no end to the tortuous road. Twisting around, the grade became steeper, hills reached up higher and higher. We were moving inland from the beachhead toward high ground that built up rapidly into the Apennines running down the center of the Peninsula, visible as a smoky, world out of reach. Wide open mouths blared out commands and threats – if I could paint a picture of a German guard it would only need an open mouth screaming torrents of abuse.

"Stinking Krauts!" The sound of my voice shouting in near delirium brought me back to full consciousness. I determined to keep a tighter hold on myself, aware that the sweating guard in front had turned and was watching me closely.

At every bend in the road we caught a glimpse of Velletri. I was stunned with the thought that we had to carry the litters all the way to Velletri and perhaps even to Rome. My outburst caused heads to turn. I was indifferent, knowing journey's end was still kilometers away; the road was steeper.

We were barely moving. When one of the prisoners collapsed the guards permitted the others to set their litters down and revive the fallen man. The concession was no evidence of compassion, there simply was no one else to take his place.

The Feldwebel was losing his composure. Heat, mud and the maddeningly slow pace finally wore through what remained of his restraint. In the beginning he had not taken any part in directing the column.

I was certain the wreck Tracy and I were carrying was near death and most of the others would follow. Suddenly, the Sergeant jabbed his Schmeizer into the ribs of the bearers, demanding more speed. His efforts were wasted since we were incapable of an extra step let alone speed and continued to move without regard for the senseless punishment.

And then, to our utter amazement, he stopped raving and quietly ordered us off the road. We milled around still carrying the wounded until one of the guards told us to rest. We walked a few paces from the group and sat down, leaning against a stonewall.

"How much farther does that crazy son-of-a-bitch think we can carry these bodies?" growled Tracy.

"It looks like Velletri."

"Fuckin' Nazis." Tracy slumped to the ground, stretched full length, his eyes closed.

"So far, we're better off than the bodies we're carrying, if that's any consolation."

"How about getting away?"

"Okay, if we're still on the road tonight, we might have a chance. We have to think about where we're going, the coast or the mountains.

Now, again, I was beyond caring. The shouts were just as loud as before, the sun was as hot and the mindless torture worsened, but I was in some strange manner observing that struggling column trudging through the steamy gray porridge.

Hysteria or amnesia, whatever my state, I was finding refuge again in a strange separation from all that was happening to me. Unaware of my disembodiment, I drifted in and out of reality.

Just above the western ridge the sun bored hard into my eyes. I closed them for a step or two before a stumble forced me to look up

I was aware of the line turning onto the dry ground of the bordering orchard and then I stretched full length beside a stone fence, gazing through scattered clouds to the perennial blue patched sky with towering cotton balls, clean and safe for a time.

The sensuous pleasure of rest was so exquisite it almost justified the hell of the ordeal made barely tolerable by the condition of the wreckage on the litters.

I touched on things far removed from my predicament. Good and bad, right and wrong, hell, the stuff drilled into you from day one. Kids get punished for doing things that are wrong, adults go to jail.

War is different, the only right is winning, and the only wrong is losing.

No matter what you believe about killing, it's been going on forever; native tribes kill their enemies, civilized people kill their enemies, heathens do it, Christians do it, who doesn't?

An old lady limped toward me using a crooked walking stick, stopping by the soldier on the litter we had been carrying. Touching the shattered boy's face, she made a clucking noise, then uncovered his legs. "Kinder..." She took an apple from her apron pocket and placed it in the soldier's hand, squeezing his fingers around it; when she released her grip, his fingers opened. She leaned down, touched his throat, moved her hand to close his eyes, straightened up and spread her hands, "Kinder kaput."

A bewildered, sad expression accompanied her feeble gesture toward the prostrate German. For a moment, she stood motionless, then made the sign of the cross and limped back along the path by the stonewall. Turning her head, she looked directly at me and broke into furious scolding; language was no barrier to her meaning.

The raucous voice of the Sergeant as he plowed through our inert bodies hammered us back into harness. As we were filing into the bog a line of horse drawn wagons brought an end to phase one of our hellish drudgery.

The Feldwebel and two Corporals engaged in another shouting match added nothing to the loading of the litters, two on each wagon crossways. They were little more than miniature imitations of the teams and vehicles I had known during my early years.

I was beginning to wonder if German non-coms had undergone throat transplants preventing them from issuing any command below the decibel level of a San Francisco foghorn.

The relief from our burden raised my spirits for a time as we walked beside the wagons, one hand on the sideboard pulling us along with a minimum of effort.

Later, approaching Velletri, we watched American fighters plummet almost to ground level, release their bombs, then climb away, reflecting the sun already setting behind the foothills and giving us a hint of hope and a large dose of envy as the planes roared away.

It was incongruous, I thought, those cowboys would be cocktailing and shouting their hits across a crowded bar on the outskirts of Naples before we would be off the road. At that moment, frustration and criticism peaked. Where I was and what was to follow was my own doing. I had pushed aside every alternative; the Army Infantry, was my choice, I had cast my fate to the wind.

When the column turned onto a hard top road on the outskirts of Velletri a noticeable raising of spirits spread through the prisoners, optimism, long buried, was reborn.

Stacy summed it up,"I've died and gone to heaven, if I'm dreaming, don't wake me up."

I responded without enthusiasm. "Our soldier boy beat you to it, no dream, it's what you think it is."

I turned to the litter; the soldier's eyes were half-closed, his lower jaw hung loose, mouth open; body muscle tension gone, he bounced and rolled with every bump.

Velletri in view, bright and shiny, streets and houses seen in the last minutes of the setting sun were tantalizingly close.

"I don't know how it'll be, but we're almost there."

Tracy's voice was low. "Pray for no moon, let's try it."

"I'm with you."

Later, as the road and orchard-vineyards faded in shadows, the roar of approaching aircraft brought a stir from guards and prisoners.

"On the left, Tracy, look, tanks – that's the target."

Fighter-bombers screamed as they pulled up and banked away, their U.S. markings on their undersides. Shattering explosions walked through orchards on both sides of the road as guards, prisoners and drivers disappeared in clouds of dust.

We crouched low as we ran through the vineyards, crashing into and tripping over vine wires strung between the fruit trees. Dust and acrid fumes hung heavy in the still night air.

I tried to hold in a sneeze that came out in a strangling eruption as shouts and commotion rose from every corner of the tank park.

I grabbed Tracy's arm. "Let's try to work around north of the road, can't chance crossing back. It's high country now, stay close."

We moved on our hands and knees through the vineyard and trees. I stopped, waiting until Tracy crawled close beside me.

"If we're separated, try to bed down before daylight. Forget trying to get through the front, keep moving up into the high country. Don't change into civilian clothes, you're United States Army, don't forget that, it carries a lot of weight regardless of what happened today. Forget being hungry and you'll live a hell of a lot longer than you think you will. Get away from here, far away – O.K., let's move."

Gradually, sounds behind us faded until the diminishing rumble from the front gave us direction. Later, vineyards behind us, we kept to the orchards, taking direction from the bordering road. I triggered a wire strung with tin cans holding iron scraps. The racket set off shouting Germans and the sound of field equipment and soldiers in a hurry.

I sprinted back into the orchard, turned left, crossed the road and ran up an open grassy slope until the shouts faded away.

Low down in the eastern blackness a small crack of light showed outlines of a building taking shape on the slope above me. I approached cautiously and circled closer until I determined the place was unoccupied. A wide door hung precariously off the bottom hinge. I waited until the rising moon revealed a pile of hay stacked to the roof in the far end. Burrowing near the back wall, I pulled the hay down around me, stretched flat on my back and fell asleep.

"Raus…"

The Corporal kicked me in the ribs, lowered his rifle and shouted again, "Raus!"

My reaction wasn't what it should have been. Blinking in the shaft of light from a loose sideboard, groggy from a deep sleep and long hours crammed with punishing, intimidating action, I was still sorting out the present when two butt blows to the rib cage got me moving.

Gasping, I struggled to my feet and staggered toward the barn door with several assists from the rifle butt and heavy boots. As they hustled me out of the barn, I learned the dimension of hate.

It burned in my throat, distorting a normal appraisal of opponents. I spit out 'master race' drawing stares and a rifle butt in the stomach, adding fuel to my loathing of a philosophy I was beginning to know but not understand.

At that moment, I was micro-seconds from losing all control, blind to my predicament and everything else in the universe, including what was to come.

In a daze, I followed the big soldier, prodded from behind when I faltered. Somewhere along that blurry trail five soldiers from Company 'B' fell in behind me.

"Lieutenant…" A rifle butt in the ribs ended the greeting.

On a hard top road we occasionally saw outlines of structures. We closed up on an open gate close to the road, entered and stopped in the yard between a two-story house and a large garage with a cement floor. A window above our heads at the far end let in moonlight.

When the door closed a soldier spoke to me. "Lieutenant, I'm Private Long, Second Platoon, Lieutenant Camden went down, mortar took him and two others. Are you all right? We have some minor wounds."

"Sorry, we never got set up, it's done with – thought I was out of it, fell asleep in a barn. We have to find a place to sit or lie down, we're ankle deep in water."

There were voices and the noise of the door scraping the ground, then a shout as four soldiers with a light entered.

"Achtung, you are Kriegsgefangenen, prisoners – Officer Hannon, out, raus."

His Corporal stripes were visible when I moved forward. He led the way across the yard to the house, up a flight of stairs. A knock on the door, it opened, I entered a large, well furnished room. A table against the back wall was set; bottles were lined up on the far side. A tall, corpulent Captain entered from a side door and sat down at the end of the table.

"American Officer – come – sit there." He pointed to a side chair.

The Corporal nudged me and pulled a chair away from the side of the table.

The German fastened a napkin to his coat and picked up a bottle. Reading the label, he said, "I am Captain Weber, a late dinner, much paperwork. Now we move forward – everything –we are Herman Goring Division, you are overmatched, our objective is the Anzio Nettuno Beachhead."

He poured a glass of wine, tasted it, and then took a long drink. A soldier placed a large tray on the table, followed by a heaping plate in front of Weber; the aroma was overwhelming. Slicing a large piece of meat, he raised it to his mouth and stopped.

"Remarkable ham."

Mouth full, he said, 'You came into the line yesterday, replacements – we know everything we need to know about Clark's Fifth Army and the 509th Parachute Battalion, a throwaway holding a center position on the front."

A long silence followed while he ate, read labels on bottles and drank. Wiping his mouth, he said, "Where is your home?"

"California."

"Oh yes, I have been there, interesting."

More eating and drinking and, suddenly, I was aware of my hunger. I hoped the Captain would offer me something, it didn't happen.

He refilled his plate and said, "I lived in New York, worked in the Foreign Division of Chase National Bank almost three years, 1936 to 1939, interesting work. The city is overrated, dominated by Jewish Bankers, the same with business manufacturers, college Professors, but then, Rosenfeld, your President is a Jew. All members of International Jewry are one in their scheme to rule the world's financial markets."

I was tired, weary to the bone, angry and tried to the limit of my endurance by Weber's offensive, crude show of superiority and the mind numbing savaging of our President and Jews. With that, I was fighting to keep my eyes open and failing – I nodded.

"So it is, war is physically hard, little rest, and now I must tell you, the war is over for you, kaput. Think about it, from here on it will be clean sheets and white bread. Remember what I say, you will find we are highly civilized people, a pure race, you will see and remember our humanity – it's time now, Lieutenant."

When the Captain stood, the guards entered and marched me back to the garage; I joined the others below the window.

"How'd it go, Lieutenant?"

"Good news, relax, Captain Weber stuffed himself with hot food and booze, told me to think about this – the war's over for us, from now on it will be 'clean sheets and white bread', that's what he said."

"Do you believe him?"

"He's a Nazi, a professional liar."

We stood under the window until weariness took over then sat down in the water and leaned against the wall. Gradually, one by one, we laid down, unmindful of anything but a need to sleep.

CHAPTER VIII

Cine Cita, the Italian Hollywood, somewhere in the eternal city of Rome. It would soon become apparent the making of motion pictures had been put on hold.

My introduction to a way of life like 'hot war' had to be lived to be understood. 'Behind the wire' said it all.

We were herded into a vast, primitive confinement on the back lot of a motion picture studio where we endured interrogation, identification and Kriegsgefangenen registration. There were long waits; sitting on the floor, standing; conversation between ourselves dried up. Depression took root, then a long night in the yard, a cup of hot tea, unquestionably ersatz.

In the early morning we were loaded into truck transports. Rumor had it our destination was a prison camp called Latterina near Florence, halfway up the boot.

Enlisted ranks and officers packed into separate cages.

Scattered in the open yard were U.S. Army Officers, British Army, Royal Air Force, U.S. Air Force; they came in all shapes and sizes, singly and in groups, standing or walking the perimeter. The yard was enclosed on three sides by double barbed wire fences sealing off the guards patrol space. A single, one-story structure hammered together out of unpainted lumber held tiers of bunks three high, an obscene latrine and single water stand pipe outside the bunkhouse.

The yard was dusty, hot and depressing.

I stood where they had pushed me through the gate. Blood had dried on my Jacket and the laceration on my arm was wrapped with a dirty bandage. Looking around, I walked to the line of prisoners carrying a variety of tin cans waiting their turn at the water spigot.

"Give up, did you?"

Bone tired, ravenous and just beginning to feel the gut-wrenching frustration of my plight, I let go with a rare display of temper. I looked at the smirking Captain, "Don't push me."

The Officer tensed, turned to face me then erupted in laughter, joined by others in earshot.

"Captain Moore, B.E.F. – you need this, hold my place."

He pushed a tin can into my hand and walked away.

Moore stepped back into line. "Water, tea, slop, whatever, this is your mess kit. How do they put you down on the roster?"

Relaxing, I turned one way and another then looked at Moore. "Thanks – Jim Hannon."

He nodded and moved forward with the line. "Two years behind the wire does things to your point of view."

"How about two days?"

Moore studied me, shambled forward to the spigot, filled his 'mess kit', and then made an exaggerated gesture toward the spigot. "Be my guest."

I crouched, holding my can under the spigot with one hand and cupped the other to splash water on my face.

Down the line a belligerent chorus erupted, "None a that shit..." "Fill your bloody can and move away." "He's takin' a fuckin' shower." "Bastard'll get a foot up 'is arse..."

I stood up, walked to the last voice and stared hard. "I'll be over there, by the fence."

Turning away, I walked to the fence and stood quietly, and drank slowly, ignoring several attempts to start a conversation. I took up the same position that evening, observing the guard's routine patrol walking between the fences.

Moore stopped by looking out across the valley sloping away from the prison. "Curfew in ten minutes."

I watched the changing of the tower guards. "How many have made it out?"

Turning to me, he said, "None, during my time there have been four attempts."

"Over the wire?"

"That's suicide; they tried to join civilian workers on their way out. Maybe you don't know – this is the back lot of a motion picture studio, Cine Cita. There is a frightening number of civil police, Fascisti, Gestapo, Wehrmacht and civilian informers around every corner. Getting out might be the least of your troubles."

He waited a moment. "I might have some advice."

"Why don't you use it?"

We walked to the barracks in silence. The interior was hot, the air fetid and foul. Thin, straw filled mattresses covered bed boards with two worn and soiled blankets rounding out the allotment.

My effort to crawl into an unoccupied bunk was rebuffed with shouted warnings from eager watchdogs.

"Taken…" "Captain Joyce's preserve…" "Go to the end, in the middle…"

I finally found a top bunk at the end, removed from windows, doors or any wayward air stream with all the foul odors and smoke packed into the dark end of the bunkhouse.

Bits of conversation came up to me from all sides.

"New Yank Leftenant's going over the wire."

"That he is – strange one."

"He'll get 'is come-uppance."

"Strikes me he'd be a handful."

Despite my anguish, I was out of it, unconscious minutes after stretching out on the flattened straw.

Stirring and turning on my back, I opened my eyes and waited, unmoving, listening and remembering. I looked around as the new day washed over the squalid surroundings. With consideration for my fellow victims, I eased down to the floor and walked over and around obstacles as heads turned and mumbled remarks, most of which went unheard.

The contrast of the contaminated atmosphere inside with the clean air moving across the yard brought me wide-awake.

I turned on the spigot and soaked my head under the stream, gulping and blowing to clear my passages. The soiled bandage disengaged giving me a sense of being whole again.

Alone in the yard, my attention was drawn to a line of assorted tin cans reaching from a spot inside the gate almost to the rear of the barracks.

After rinsing my mess kit, I walked to the head of the line and stood in place as a two-wheel cart pulled by two guards reached the gate. A large, metal container sent off wisps of steam. I looked back as prisoners, one by one, left the barracks and took positions at varying intervals along the line.

Remarks grew in volume: "Who's the bugger at the head of the line?" "What the hell does he think he's doin'?" "Hey mate, go to the back of the line."

The precise beat of clumping boots striking the ground in measured cadence caused me to turn as the sound closed and stopped close to one side.

Battle dress, shirt, tie, beret at a jaunty angle, bristling R.A.F. mustache and fierce, righteous glare added up to an incensed British Major. His stare was on a level with mine.

Assuming a ramrod straight position, annoyingly close, obviously designed to intimidate, he barked, "What's the meaning of this?" His voice was much too loud.

"There was no one here, a line of tin cans, so here I am."

"Major Duncan, your name?"

The wet breath, delivered from a position not more than six inches from my face, was decidedly unpleasant.

"Would you mind stepping back?"

A long pause as the Major's jaw worked furiously and his face became flushed; almost imperceptibly, he moved back.

"Thanks – Lieutenant Jim Hannon."

"Leftenant, I'll overlook your insubordination inasmuch as you are new here. Go to the end of the line."

During the Major's performance, guards had positioned the cart directly behind me. I stepped to one side, held out my tin can, received a splash of what passed for hot tea and moved toward the fence as the Major, using his patented parade ground voice that probably tumbled young ladies out of bed in the seminary across the valley shouted his warning.

"Leftenant Hannon, you will be on report, this date, for gross insubordination."

I walked toward the fence where I stood looking through the wire, sipping the ersatz tea as thin wisps of smoke rose straight up from scores of chimney pots in the awakening valley.

The noise of trucks in low gear rose in volume as they approached, then stopped in line at the gate of our compound.

A Wermacht Captain led a platoon into the yard where they took up positions around the perimeter holding their rifles at port arms, the ready position. He shouted into the barracks, flushing out a rumpled

British Colonel not yet fully awake and the warmed up Major Duncan followed by a U.S. 45th Division Major and a Lieutenant wearing a 3rd Division shoulder patch.

In minutes the inmates were in ranks, British on the right, U.S. on the left. Major Duncan marched front center and addressed the assembled prisoners.

"You are moving out, transport by rail, gather your personal kit. You have ten, repeat, ten minutes, reassemble as you were. Dismiss."

Standing in a front file, I heard the Colonel say "Twenty minutes." I expressed my thoughts without any attempt to mute my voice, "Major Duncan, the kind that must have invented military agony, hurry up and wait."

* * *

We counted off, twenty to a car, filed past a row of tables, received a loaf of bread and a blanket, were loaded up and herded into one end of the car by four guards who would ride with us to the unannounced destination.

Straw covered the floor, a bucket against the sidewall served as latrine. When the chain fence barrier was secured across the open end, the prisoners shared less than one-half of the car.

The door slid into place, a whistle blew and the train started with a jerk. I stood in a corner at the end of the car, packed in by those standing, crouching and sitting. An oil lamp hanging in the guard's quarters sent out enough light to reveal all of the details and the click of wheels striking rail joints indicated our speed. As the day wound down, pencils of light visible around the doors gradually disappeared.

The first long night, like so many preceding it, was a new experience. Loaves of bread appeared here and there; conversation was little more than a whisper. A hard-faced Corporal and Private, automatic weapons across their knees, sat on bales of straw facing the prisoners.

A reflector on one side of the lamp left the guard's area in deep shadow, throwing most of the light on the opposite end.

Lieutenant Samuels, standing beside me, began sliding to the floor. I managed to get an arm around him. Slight and uncommonly quiet, his outward demeanor was cheerful despite his wasted appearance.

"What's the problem?"

Samuels shook his head. Eyes closed, he slumped against me; I moved out of the corner and lowered him to the floor.

"Don't crowd, let me pass." I worked my way toward the wire, then across the car and stopped. The first three men to load, by design, had staked out a claim, sprawling, full length, side by side, arms loose at their sides, legs comfortably spread, blankets rolled up for headrests, enjoying a private joke when I interrupted.

"It isn't going to work."

They looked at me, blank eyed and indifferent. The man in the middle, Captain Goode, was smiling as he nudged the other two.

"You talking to me?"

"I'm talking to the three of you, look around, there are men standing since we boarded. We're going to share space and that means all of us, hope you enjoyed your rest. Sit up, back up, and pull in your legs."

There was no response other than amused stares until I stomped down hard on the Captain's shin.

"You son-of-a-bitch..." He came up reaching and ran into a short punch slamming him against the side of the car. He dropped to the floor as the other two pulled tight beside him, legs drawn up. A small cheer ran through the packed prisoners.

I turned away and froze, the Corporal's pale blue, hard eyes were open wide, his weapon pointed at me inches from the wire; a quick motion of his terminated the crisis. I moved back to the corner beside Samuels.

Dozing, waking, sitting, wondering – a weird sameness put everyone on hold. Rank was meaningless; guards changed, the replacements older, talking loud with bursts of laughter. It seemed they ate constantly, chewed something and threw it in a bucket half-consumed. Their purpose was obvious; the bucket was close to the wire.

I stood, stretched, flexed my muscles then crouched and rolled Samuels on his other side.

He opened his eyes, smiled and whispered, "Day?"

"Harry just marked nine on the sideboard. Want some good news?"

He nodded.

"Nine bad ones behind us. No matter how you count, we're nine days closer to home."

He squeezed my hand and closed his eyes.

The train slowed and stopped and we were unloaded. Unshaven, grimy, endurance and spirit almost gone, the debilitating effects of confinement and starvation rations were revealed.

With guards leading and trailing, we marched away in three ranks while local people stood mute watching us pass.

Someone shouted, "Your new rest home, Schubin, Poland, Oflag 64."

CHAPTER IX

In early January there was a noticeable quickening of interest in the developments on the eastern front. We were aware of Russians massing unprecedented numbers of armor, infantry and artillery divisions in various places along the winter line, the Vistula River

In keeping with the news, the spirit of the camp as a whole rose in anticipation of rescue. Events moved into high gear on both fronts; we could scarcely sleep waiting for the news. The opening of the great attack from the east was to be launched momentarily.

Before lights out the cubicle reader of news gathered from all sources including German, read a brief summary.

"Today Russian airmen dropped leaflets throughout eastern Poland. They carried a brief message, three words, 'Roggosovski is coming." Whistles and shouts sounded throughout the barracks. Sleep was long in coming.

And then it happened!

Our mingled hopes and fears were materializing in a sudden frenzy of activity instigated by a command from the German Oberst that the camp would be evacuated. The movement was to be executed on foot, destination undisclosed.

A Russian breakthrough of unprecedented proportions was collapsing and overrunning the entire winter line of the eastern front. From a point just north of Cracow to another in distant Lithuania on the Baltic, a line of natural and man made barricades had been breached by a massive artillery preparation followed by the launching of armies, armor and infantry.

What could be seen of the surrounding country was devoid of life. The usual chimney smoke from the cookhouse, the German's guard's quarters and the surrounding farmhouses had ceased. An ominous silence engulfed the slightly rolling farmlands from horizon to horizon. The road paralleling the front of the prison camp, packed for three days and nights with an endless stream of Hitler's settlers, was empty.

I had been unable to feel any compassion for that frantic mass of desperate refugees. They invoked nothing more than a feeling of curiosity or a silent prayer of thanks for not being one of them. In turn, they seemed unmindful of the sprawled bodies and pitiful possessions littering both ditches. They were alive for the moment, striving to reach the Fatherland, and the Fatherland seemed to be fleeing from the onrushing horde of refugees. I wondered at the contradiction posed by the disintegration of the 'New Order' that was to have ruled for a thousand years.

I remembered a long conversation with Francois Bissette, a French Infantry Captain, quartered in an adjacent barracks in Oflag 64 who had gone underground in Paris after the French surrender. He escaped to Algiers, joined the Free French Army and fought with the Fifth Army in Italy before becoming a prisoner. He talked long and passionately about the Nazis, his hatred was uncontained.

"During the years of occupation, to be a German set one above other people. To be a German meant great power and prestige for them and undisputed advantages and privileges. Then, their fanatic devotion to their leader and to each other had been the wonder of the world and a basic reason for their success. Out of their military achievements had been born a fierce, intense pride and belief in their racial superiority.

"For them there had been two distinct classes or races in the world, those who could boast of German blood and those who could not. If you belonged to the latter category you must accept that fact and by no means act or, by inference, offend the Herrenvolk. On the other hand, if you were German you would, by every act and manner, make known that fact and make all others understand that an offense against yourself or any one of your countrymen would be considered an overt act against all Germans who would, in due course, punish the offender; gas him, shoot him, starve and beat him, his family and friends. In so doing be certain that he and all who were to be impressed knew the offender was being punished by a German or someone who had been appointed by Germans for an offense against Germans. The word 'German' must be understood by all of those who were privileged to call themselves German and should be treated with reverence. Their special privilege and position was their birthright, not to be questioned."

For three days and nights a desperate column had been passing. What had become of their fierce allegiance and comradeship that supposedly belonged only to Germans? Bodies removed from crowded wagons were not tenderly lowered to the ground and covered with snow in some semblance of respect, they had simply been handed down while the wagon remained in motion, placed in a ditch and abandoned. Those walking, young and old, pled in vain for a place in wagons, carriages or on the backs of horses and cattle.

Those who were riding ignored those on foot and cursed wagons in front of them for not moving faster. Others who begged and cried for help from ditches and shoulders of the road were ignored and cursed drivers for refusing their pleas.

Earlier, as the desperate mob crawled by, Bissette talked or thought aloud, "So, now it's back to the Fatherland, to the 'Thousand Year Reich'. You have a surprise coming if you get there, the shining cities aren't there anymore, they're gone, kaput, la vie est breve, c'est triste, sooner than you think, a few days, maybe hours and the thunder from the east will roll over you like a tidal wave."

I looked at the Frenchman. "You feel no pity for them?"

Bissette faced me, anger in his voice, "Do you?"

"Maybe the little ones."

The Frenchman looked back to the road. "My sympathy is all used up for the little ones they put in Buchenwald, Dachau, Tremblenki, Maidonek, Auschwitz and a thousand silent places. They should pay for every drop of blood, for every tear, for every hour of loneliness. That was written by a Russian journalist when he stood trying to comprehend the purpose, the enormity of the German obscenity unleashed at Babi Yar in the Russian Crimea."

The order was given to the prisoners in early morning and was followed by all day preparations. I watched the others absorbed in their packing and speculation while observing the frantic efforts of the guards to hurry the process. Growing sounds of fighting to north and east caused an ominous chill and sense of foreboding until I saw the opportunity; moving carefully, I found a secure alcove in the hospital supply room. The old structure shot out rifle cracks as frost squeezed the timbers.

I reasoned that the guards would have little time to search for anyone not answering roll call. In the early evening, when ranks were being formed, amidst the shouting and confusion, I slipped into the shadows and made my way unnoticed to the third floor via seldom used back stairs. Standing on the railing, I forced a hatch in the ceiling, pulled myself through the hole, replaced the cover and carefully worked my way across rafters to a spot near the eaves at the front of the building. There, I lay quietly alert, knowing by the sounds when the columns were finally formed, watching them march out of camp. The cold was intense, causing me to tighten cramping muscles and beat my arms against my body.

Long after the decreasing noise of shouted commands and marching died away, I climbed down and surveyed the scene. A number of bed-patient prisoners had been left behind in the infirmary; an American doctor and several other officers were permitted to remain in charge of the camp.

I resisted a strong impulse to shout; the silence and freedom was intoxicating. It came to me that I was still a prisoner and that the threat of a German counterattack or a retreating force overrunning the camp removed my options.

Opening the gate, I walked out of the camp and stood there, taking it all in; the 'Big House', lines of barracks, assembly field, debris scattered where prisoners had formed ranks – not one solitary sign of life, the camp was a ghost town. I turned away.

The sun was bright and unseasonably warm, trees were dazzling with a heavy coat of hoarfrost and a surface crust of shiny snow spread out across the fields. German barracks and the Oberst's house with doors and smokeless chimneys seemed unreal. The front door of the supply shed was open; I crossed the road and entered. Red Cross food boxes were stacked floor to ceiling along the sidewall. I filled my pockets with Lucky Strike cigarettes and emergency ration Hershey bars. Marveling at the abundance of treasures, I stood a moment then walked out and turned east.

Toward the town of Rembertov, where the road turned, there was no sign of vehicles or people. Without apprehension I started walking, not knowing how I would respond to a hostile reception from the Russians or whoever occupied the town.

The by-products of the exodus that had been passing for days soon began to be distinguished between bundles of clothing or bedding and other inert shapes that were probably the result of bursts of automatic weapons the night before. The bodies were civilian, invariably in a ditch or sprawled on the shoulder of the road.

With mixed emotions, I felt they had stretched their luck, waited too long, their Wermacht smashed, loyal burghers chased, hunted and left to die without so much as a stone marker.

I stopped to look at a corpse covered from neck to ankles in an enormous black Persian lamb coat, the upturned hem and collar trimmed with a brown, smooth fur. Arms outstretched, eyes partially open, there were no visible wounds or signs of violence.

"I should trade coats, no way he'll be buried in it."

Attracted by heavy motor sounds, I continued to walk toward town.

CHAPTER X

Alert and tense, I approached around a curve, past scattered small houses and outbuildings; debris in the ditches had dwindled to an occasional mattress or bundle of clothing.

The absence of life, human or animal, and their small sounds was disquieting. I was debating whether to go on or turn back when the road straightened. I saw soldiers spreading across the road, weapons in hand and continued walking until I closed the interval and said, "Soldier, American, U.S.A."

They gave no sign as they closed around me muttering strange words, impressing me with their inscrutable Asiatic features and phyletic sameness.

I pointed to a truck, then fixed my eyes on the man nearest, slowly enunciating, "Stew-dee-bach-her – da?"

Grins broke the sober faces and a lessening of the tension until a hard-faced soldier pushed through, held out his hand and demanded, "Documente."

My pantomime coupled with mixed English, German and, a wild guess pulled out of memory, had a positive effect.

"Amerikanski – Tedeschi Lager – Nyet documente."

While the Russians exchanged views, I eased out a pack of cigarettes, lit one, blew out the fragrant smoke and offered the pack to the man who had demanded documents.

Never taking his eyes off me, he extracted a cigarette, accepted a light and nodded. I passed the pack around watching the ritual of lighting, inhaling, exhaling, smiles and enthusiastic endorsements.

"Ou-ss-ah – karasha…" Suddenly, in response to a distant shout, they boarded the truck, waved, shouted, held out their cigarettes and were gone.

Gathered in town were four huge tanks parked so their long barreled cannon covered every avenue of approach.

A group loitering under the cannon pointed in my direction, and watched me approach. Long black cloaks fastened at the throat, black aviator type helmets and knee-length-felt boots had an unsettling effect. My confidence lessened as I closed the interval.

"Anglisher?"

A tall, thin soldier with a single striped epaulet on his shoulder held a chunk of black bread in one hand and a square of bacon fat in the other.

"Amerikanski…" My voice was more resolute than I felt.

The whole climate of the encounter, exaggerated by the theatrical garb of the silent Russians eroded my confidence and vocabulary.

Soldiers from the other tanks joined the crowd. A face with an ugly, livid scar cutting diagonally above the left eyebrow, across the bridge of the nose and down to the jawbone was inches from me.

"Tedeschi." It was an unmistakable accusation.

Staring straight into the black eyes I waited for a moment then slowly raised my left arm with my sliver bracelet around my wrist.

"Ou-ss-ah – Amerikanski Officer."

Shouting from the back of a tank opened a lane revealing a tall Officer; he motioned me to join him.

A loaf of black bread, slab of bacon fat and straw covered bottle were sitting on a flat place at the rear of the tank. Someone thrust a chunk of bread at me, another extended a square of bacon fat on the point of a knife. Their faces had lost their hard looks; most of the conversation was directed at me. I smiled, took both offerings and bit into the sour bread.

Holding the bread in one hand, I offered a pack of cigarettes, pushed them toward the Officer and spoke the magic line, Ou-ss-ah, motioning with my free hand around the circle.

A heavy jug was propelled from the back of the tank into my arms. A pungent odor spilled out of the open top, I guessed it was Vodka.

The Lucky Strikes were a hit, held out and hailed with a torrent of Russian interspersed with "Ou-ss-ah" and signs that I drink.

The large opening gushed, filling my mouth to overflowing causing me to gasp and gulp air, then cough and hand off the bottle while my audience laughed and signaled me to try again.

Aware that their interest had shifted to something in back of me, I turned my head, spun around and watched as a long column of German prisoners approached four abreast.

They showed familiar signs – uncertain, worn out, with a hunted look, not knowing what was to come.

Some were bandaged, some limped, and others struggled on makeshift crutches. All were unshaven, desperate men carrying bundles slung on their backs, the total of their worldly goods, going out of the world, as most of them were, with pitifully little more than they had brought into it.

As I looked at individuals, my thankfulness for not being one of them obliterated my building animosity I harbored for those who had invaded other's homelands, people who had not in their lifetime wanted anything more than to be left alone.

The dispossessors had become the dispossessed. It was as it should be, the scales would be balanced and, in that same instant, I knew they never had been and there was little evidence in my view of things they ever would be.

When the column closed up suddenly, as marching men do, the prisoners stumbled, churned about and stopped.

My eyes locked on those of the man directly opposite me. A soiled scarf wrapped around served as a headpiece. Pale blue eyes glared at me as though the prisoner had found the cause of his trouble. My voice was audible to those around me, "It's a roll of the dice."

Shouts up and down the road started the column moving. Before he was blocked from view, the German turned his head, stared hard at me, stumbled and was out of sight.

The tankers loaded up; engines rumbling, they moved onto the intersecting road to the west.

As the winter night closed in, the quick wind caused me to pause, thinking of the long green line marching to what?

"Jim, you son-of-a-bitch!"

Teel grabbed me from behind. The roughneck's eyes were actually misty, his voice choked.

"They were in a hurry. After rest stops the count was sloppy, Captain Fleuger ordered a quick search of houses and barns and away we went. Hell, we were makin' maybe one or two miles an hour; the guards would go into a huddle, shout at us to shape up, they were downright nervous and plenty scared.

"Three o'clock we pulled off the road – lots of stables, corrals and piles of hay. Some of the Kriegies, maybe twenty or thirty, found hiding places; I climbed a pile of baled hay in the stable, found a space on top, pulled a bale over me, waited till the sounds faded away and walked back. I think there'll be more showin' up."

I stared at the lowering clouds.

"Somethin' botherin' you?"

" I'm leavin' in the morning, going east, come along if you like."

"East? You may be right, no way to get through the other way."

"That's it, let's go back to camp for tonight, it's too late to find a nest."

* * *

Captain Harry Jensen, Medical Corps, seemed to be enjoying his own brand of humor as he plopped into a chair and put his feet on the table.

"I overheard you two plotting, so, I'm butting in, quit dreaming, I'm issuing orders; no one will be permitted to leave camp until proper authority takes over, U.S., British, Russian…"

"German." I interrupted.

"Ha, ha." Jensen's thin smile vanished.

Supply rooms had been broken open providing a mountain of Red Cross food packages; assorted items were on the table.

"We'll stay here, that's an order. Locks are back on supplies, all items will be rationed until the big picture is clarified. I have assigned duties, you two are on guard tonight, two hours on and two off; your station will be the German guard tower at the main gate. That, gentlemen, is the way it is." Jensen made a thing of what he considered a command.

Teel leaned across the table, "Knock it off, leave us out of your war games."

"No one, Lieutenant, leaves here, I am the senior officer and responsible for the hospital patients who, incidentally, are the only people authorized to be here."

54

I pulled an unopened carton of cigarettes closer, opened it, removed a pack, lit a cigarette and gave Jensen an appraising look.

"There is an open carton and an open pack on the table, any reason you opened another?"

"Captain, tomorrow morning it's over. I volunteer to stand guard, if Teel feels the same, we'll spell each other."

"Are you refusing my orders?"

I stood up. "I'll take the first watch. Look around, Pat, we need a backpack or a bindle and I need a winter coat. We'll take the duty until midnight."

"Then what?"

"Bedtime."

"Midnight?"

"You heard right, midnight."

Captain Jensen looked from one to the other. "O.K., these are combat conditions, you're facing Leavenworth."

Teel slapped the table. "I can't believe this guy, one hour shifts, O.K."

"That'll do it."

* * *

We opened the gate, turned and looked at the hospital, the 'big house', the rows of barracks, guard towers and strip of ground running next to the inner fence. Warning signs stuck on the fence proclaimed 'OUT OF BOUNDS – GUARDS WILL SHOOT – OUT OF BOUNDS!' we turned and walked out.

The air was still, the sun bright in a cloudless sky; thick frost and snow crunched and squeaked under foot. I could feel the cold biting my throat and lungs.

Bare trees, fences and brush lining the ditch were ablaze with frost crystals reflecting the sunlight in a dazzling, blinding glare, forcing us to continuously wipe away tears from our eyes. Bodies along the road had been stripped of shoes and outer garments.

"See that big one in the underwear? Right over there. Yesterday, he was the best dressed man I saw all day."

On the main street there were a number of abandoned and looted stores and shops. A small shop displayed a few loaves of bread, some buns and pieces of sausage; a short, bald-headed man came to the door.

"Hello boys, where you go? You from camp, yes?" He extended his hand.

"My name's Jesionowski, Cyna Jesionowski, I was long time in America, in Peetsbourg, Noo Jork, Deetroit. You come now – have something." He motioned for us to sit down at a marble topped table much like an old-fashioned ice cream parlor in one of the small towns back home, put several glasses and a bottle on the table.

"Is not so good as before, this, Russians like – bah! Before war, nobody drink this."

"Okay, Pop," Teel laughed and winked at me. "We'll have to take it easy, it's been a long time. Good luck."

We raised our glasses; Jesionowski pulled up a chair and sat down as the room filled with people. Each time any words passed between us, he translated for the bystanders who, with great urgency, spoke to him – he waved his hand impatiently.

"Questions, questions, they want to know everything – everybody here likes Americans. Ah…" he sighed, "…America is good, always here troubles, we are poor, Germans take everything."

He fumbled around inside his coat, pulled out a fat wad of papers, searched through them then proudly drew out one and spread it on the table.

"My American paper, I was almost citizen. My family was citizen, now, I don't know. You see, my name here, Cyna Jesionowski. Where your home?"

"San Francisco, Lieutenant Teel is from New York."

"When did you leave America?" Teel asked.

"Before war, ten years, my wife was sick and our people were here.

"The older boy, he would not come. It is now six years since a letter comes." He made a kind of resigned motion with his hands.

"My family, three years now they went to Cracow because to stay here not possible. We have nothing. They went to farm of my brother. Maybe now, soon, I will get letter."

"What about all of these stores and big houses with the broken windows?"

The old man looked solemnly at the table, then spoke softly, "Germans and Poles, there were some. You must understand, to be a Pole was to have nothing. Always Germans want more and more. Today a cow, tomorrow a horse, flour and even clothes and furniture, your house and land. This Poland, here, was under Government General, the Nazis, and soon come German people. You have store, mill or farm – they come say..." the old man's chin was quivering. His voice lost the softness, his fists tightly clenched on the table.

"They say, 'Raus, get out now!' In minutes you must go and what you can carry only. Where you are to go? Not to take one horse and wagon, just go – 'Raus'! And these not SS men, these German people, farmers, shopkeepers. You have two houses do they say, 'you go and live in the small one?' No, no, they take everything, you must go, all the time shouting, walking around, pointing to things, 'This you cannot take, and this, and this.' You say, 'Where am I to go, my children and my things?' They scream more loud and strike. My wife said, 'No, this our home, you have no right!' they strike her."

He stopped talking and gestured hopelessly with his hands, tears fell unnoticed on the back of his hand. He wiped his eyes with his coat sleeve.

After a moment, Teel spoke quietly, "You won't forget the Germans." It was well meant, but brought an angry response.

Jesionowski raised his head. "We never forget Germans." Then he was on his feet, pounding the table and shouting, "Could anyone forget Germans?" He glared at the startled people filling his shop.

Several of them edged slowly toward the door as he sat down heavily and talked some more. "So, not to be German, very hard, many people signed paper, give up being Poles. Paper say this man – woman, so and so, swears to be German, swears to be Nazi. Germans permit them who sign to have store or farm, to keep their place. Some were bad, like Germans, because they know they are traitors, they know what we feel. They are shamed so they try harder to please Germans, they have little more things, little more freedom for a while."

"Are you a Jew? Was that the reason, or did it matter?' I knew it mattered.

"Not Jew, Jews we had few, not many. You are Jew, you are gone, all family, with nothing to take, gone in one hour.

57

"Because you not German, you are punished. They say Jew is Communist, they say Pole who will not sign paper are Communists, I am not Communist. Yes, it is worse to be Jew, all Jews were sent away, but if you are not Jew, just Pole and not want to be German you are in danger, much danger. Many Polish peoples are taken away."

He turned to Teel. "No, no, never forget German." Waving his finger he said, "Maybe in America is hard for people to know what these devils do, you tell them."

Suddenly, he stopped talking and reached for his glass. We picked up our drinks; the glasses were empty when we placed them back on the table.

Teel shifted his feet and pushed his chair back, "We have to keep moving, Pop. Thanks for the drink, I hope you find your family soon." He paused for a moment. "Don't worry about us forgetting the Germans, we have things to remember."

We stood up and shook hands with Jesionowski and the others in turn.

CHAPTER XI

The days passed, endless hours were made more ominous by the dark sky hugging the ground and an icy wind straight out of the north. Except for a military vehicle speeding west and a small group of silent and remote dwellings and outbuildings half-buried in the snow, the country appeared deserted.

Late morning, after we had fallen into a long silence, a Russian Army truck stopped and took us aboard. For the first time, the miles raced past. We didn't notice the cold at first sitting close to the tailgate comparing, with soaring spirits, the speed of the truck with our efforts on foot. The road spewing out behind was constantly turning and rolling up and down short, steep hills. With a numbing frost transmitted from the steel floor to our feet and the cold creeping higher, our enthusiasm hit the wall.

"We've made our quota for the day, I could be talked into walking." Teel's voice was heavy with fatigue.

"Let's hang on, looks like a storm."

In minutes a heavy, white curtain of snow shut out the view. Hours later, the truck pulled to the left side of the road and moved along in low gear.

I twisted my body until I could see over the tailgate. A wretched looking column of German prisoners stumbling in the deep snow with heads bowed into the wind, were indifferent to the truck or the Red soldiers herding them out of the way. Without a word we watched them pass.

They would have much on their minds in addition to the bitter cold, I thought; uncertainty, the void to the east, the people, Poles and Russians, who would look into their eyes as though searching for one man in particular.

A sharp gust of wind ballooned the skirts of their long greatcoats. Momentarily the prisoners halted and hunched their shoulders, then moved on, vanishing in the swirling snow as the truck moved back to the center of the road and picked up speed.

After a long run, we turned off the road across open country, occasionally backing up to start again and plow through soft spots. Visibility was almost zero.

We dozed until the truck stopped with a lurch; the unusual quiet and lack of motion brought us awake, alert and apprehensive.

"Let's go."

Jumping over the tailgate, we walked to the front of the truck where the Russians were studying the situation; both front wheels were in a hole.

"Cigarette?"

They looked at Teel for a moment, accepted cigarettes, both smiled and one spoke. Though we had been riding for hours, the Russians had not displayed any curiosity, now it was obvious we were subjects of the conversation. I said, "Amerikanski," pointing to Teel and myself.

Surprised, they repeated as though they were dubious. "Amerikanski?"

"Da, da." Teel answered.

"Panimayish Russki?"

I shook my head. Teel made an attempt to show we wanted to help.

The driver walked to the back of the truck and returned with shovels. Together we cleared the snow from behind the front wheels and chopped ice that was preventing any play backward or forward. The driver examined front and back wheels, nodded, climbed in the cab and started the motor. We watched, wondering if he could work the front wheels out of the hole. He put the truck in gear, carefully moved back, then, catching it on the short roll, stepped down hard on the throttle moving the truck out of the hole.

Teel shouted and held up his fist. "Good driver, Karasha."

The Russians grinned as the second one climbed into the cab. I shook my head and walked across the field ahead of the truck, testing the snow and searching out the best route. Just before dark a village west of our course drew the driver's attention.

We led the truck around one end of the village, then stepped on the running board. The driver pulled up in front of the largest house and shut off the motor. We circled the house, approached the entrance, stood for a moment, pushed open the door and entered.

Later, in response to my question, the driver placed a sheet of paper on the table and drew a sketch of Western Poland, placing dots for Warsaw, Bromberg and Poznan. When he located our position we whistled in amazement. Apparently, the truck, after leaving the road, had traveled almost straight south, putting us miles off our planned course. He explained they had by-passed German units in the area. Poznan was putting up a desperate fight and the city was completely surrounded. Germans, in small groups were working their way toward Poznan and in a matter of days or a week or two the city would fall. The reason for the route they had taken was to avoid any area not known to be in Russian hands. Between their location and the Bromberg-Warsaw Highway there were known to be many enemy pockets.

Finally, the combination of fatigue, spirits and stuffy warmth was too much. In a hazy stupor we were led to an alcove filled wall to wall with a sleeping platform where we collapsed and were asleep in seconds.

In the morning the aroma of frying ham permeated the room. We hurried outside, washed quickly and returned to the house in high spirits. The farmer pointed to the table.

"It's a beautiful day." Teel turned away from the window. "Where are the soldiers?"

"Left early this morning, we're alone with the family, I don't like it, drop the questions, Pat."

"Why did they leave without us?"

I pointed toward the kitchen. "The man told me to stay on this road through the center of town. Twenty kilometers north we'll reach – I've forgotten the name – it doesn't matter, it's the first city."

Our smiling host placed two plates on the table loaded with slices of ham and potatoes.

"Incredible."

"Shall I give him some Luckies?"

"When we thank him. By the way, where are we going?"

Teel laughed and shook his head. "I haven't the foggiest idea, how about Moscow?"

"Could be, doesn't really matter, just so the guns are on our right and we keep moving."

* * *

We lost track of time, moving with a single purpose, to get on, just get on. Hour after hour we walked, hoping every turn of the road would have an answer to our dilemma. There were no villages; now and then we passed farmhouses, if occupied the people gave no sign. The air was still, unnaturally quiet and the reflection of the sun off the snow had become a problem.

Some time after mid-day, a small village poked up out of the unbroken, white blanket. Approaching cautiously, everything appeared peaceful and still, yet I felt uneasy. As we passed the first houses the feeling began to lift. Halfway through the village, turning a right angle corner, we saw them.

Four Germans, close to the houses, walked toward us. Committed to the center of the road, we continued walking. I whispered, "Don't talk, don't look."

The Germans stopped and watched us approach; one carried a light machine gun and belts of ammunition draped over his shoulder; the others had Schmeizers. The lowered guns stayed on us as the distance closed.

Trying not to stare or turn our heads, we took in every detail; the hard, unshaven faces, a bandaged hand, a fur Jacket visible under one open greatcoat, green fur-trimmed hats and the automatic weapons.

Very close now, the Germans waited; we continued to walk forward. As they came abreast we saw them turning to face us, then they were out of sight.

I had never stepped more carefully, nor had high noon been more ominously quiet other than the one sound we tried desperately to avoid – our boots rhythmically crushed the dry, fresh snow with a squeaky, crunching sound. The noise jeopardized our efforts to play out the scene, the deadly, now unseen enemy frozen in place. We saw the corner where the road turned sharply to the left. Just past the third house, the world stopped in an unreal silence. My foggy breath was sending a signal that could bring shattering fire.

A hot, itching feeling on my scalp and neck needed scratching, my eyes were watering, causing objects at hand to lose form. The urge to turn my head and look back was overwhelming, as was my determination not to do anything that might provoke those grim, desperate soldiers. Why was it taking so long to reach the corner?

Our lives could end any second. Again I fought a strong impulse to turn and look. Maybe I should have spoken, a nod of recognition or a word. No matter, it was too late for anything but the drama playing out in an obscure Polish crossroads, known only to those frozen in place for a moment in time.

We were closing on the corner past the third house, if we could reach it, we could make a run for it. I had a feeling people were watching. We finally reached the corner, turned and risked a glance back down the street.

The enemy had turned, their weapons were still on us. Then the corner of a house came between us and we broke into a run. We turned between two houses and followed a fence line back to a road. We stopped and stood, catching our breath.

I spoke as I looked back to the point where the road disappeared.

"Believe in angels."

"Why not?"

The road was out in the open now. Neither of us wanted to break the silence, acutely aware of the line that could have closed out our service record – 'missing in action'. We held our pace.

Just before the sun sank into the shadows the unmistakable haze and heavy smoke marked a place where people were working and smokestacks were belching.

"Do you see it?"

"See what?"

"The city, that black cloud hugging the ground."

"Another surprise, what do you think?"

"I think we'll soon know."

Barren and seemingly abandoned country gave me concern. People in big numbers gave a feeling of security; perhaps it was a kind of herd instinct. Thousands living in a small area mathematically reduces any threat to the lives of one or two, I believed that.

After dark, we entered the city, walking unnoticed among the few hurrying shadows. There were no lights and, until our eyes became accustomed to the darkness, we collided with obstacles and people. Before we could make amends, the person would be swallowed up in the dark.

Structures changed from one level to two – we agreed it was time to find shelter.

"Let's try one."

Teel took the lead, feeling his way along a wall until he found a gate, stopped, knocked and, after a short wait, opened it and stepped inside, calling out 'Pani', 'Panyinka'.

Suddenly shouts and sounds of scuffling shattered the silence. As I felt my way forward, rough hands fastened on my shoulders; I was thrown violently against a wall shouting, "Amerikanski, Amerikanski!" The noise of the struggle resounded off the walls as our assailants hit with their fists and clubbed with rifle butts.

The attack ceased as quickly as it had begun; hands that had been striking were holding me upright. One voice sounded over, loud and scalding.

Offering no resistance, we were herded from the courtyard into the building, up a flight of stairs and along a hall. A door opened and we were pushed into a shadowy area dimly lit from an adjoining room, then dragged through an open door and slammed down on a sofa.

Soldiers crowded in shouting and pushing close. They were heavily armed, and wore caps with short bills and triangular fronts and unidentifiable uniforms.

"What the hell are they?"

"Here comes your answer, Pat."

The crowd stirred at a word from a short, stocky officer wearing thick, horned rimmed glasses who was working his way toward us. He saluted formally, a sort of three fingered gesture accompanied by a quick bow.

"Fortunately for you," he said, "I understand English."

He looked at me, "It's a good thing you shouted, otherwise my men might have killed you before I could stop them." He laughed.

We smiled and waited.

The officer spoke again, "I'm Captain Kalo. We are a Polish Division attached to the Russian Army here in Strykow. Many Germans are still in this city and many more are attempting to hide in the surrounding country. We have been here two days and still we find them. At night they are more bold and so, when my men spoke to you, well, you did not answer properly. I hope you are not hurt."

Teel answered, "A few bruises, that's all right."

"Do you have any papers?" He was looking at me.

"No papers." I explained, "We're American Officers, German prisoners for more than a year, we have no documents."

I unfastened my bracelet. "Here, you see my name, Lieutenant Jim Hannon and my number, my United States Army Serial Number; that is all the proof we have."

Kalo handed back the bracelet, saluted and left the room.

I lit a cigarette, offered Teel one and waited until the smoke floated around the room, then held out the pack. Stern faces widened into smiles. No one refused and when Teel got across the word 'America', the crisis was over.

A young soldier made his way into the room and motioned for us to follow. In total darkness we made our way up another flight of stairs; our guide knocked on a door with long vertical cracks revealing slivers of light.

A thin, elderly civilian in pants and an undershirt opened the door, led us to a bedroom then bowed out quickly. I dropped wearily beside Teel who had stretched out on the bed and closed his eyes. For the moment, perhaps all night, we might be secure. Occasionally, we heard rifle shots, sometimes accompanied with shouts; the deadly game went on and on.

A new day was almost at the halfway mark when someone knocked timidly. A young man entered with a tray of sliced bread, white fat and hot tea. We consumed every morsel, dressed hurriedly, thanked our host and made our way downstairs. Finding no one around, we left.

We continued along the street, anxious to reach open country, feeling confident as the clear sky and warming sun gave hope for our day-to-day hit and miss search.

At a distance, a crowd of people had gathered, shouting at something obscure. We saw a cage fashioned out of peeled logs placed on one side of the street. A man sat inside dressed in his underwear, his bare feet and hands purple with cold, his face swollen and discolored. Sitting cross-legged, stupefied, as though he could not feel the cold or pain, he seemed remote, unaware of his shocking condition.

I answered everyone who questioned us with one word, "Amerikanski," and we soon became the center of attention. An old man shoved through the crowd. He told us he had lived in America and asked the usual questions, translating for the others who exclaimed at every remark. I slowed him down long enough to ask a question in turn, "Who is that?"

"Ah, him," the old man answered, glancing toward the cage. "He was German Commandant of this city, Strykow. Germans were killed or taken away; the people ask to have this man to punish and this is how they do it. Each man who suffered because of him can come here, look at him and say, 'Remember me, Herr Kommandant?'"

He turned to the cage and shouted, "My name is Ludsuski, my father and brother you killed – so many things in five years he did, hardly anyone in this city could not accuse him.

"Do you know these Germans, Lieutenant? What they have done to the people? We are not able to punish him enough to satisfy everyone. Two days he is there, the longer he lives the more he remembers. No food, no water, he stays so until finished."

He shouted something that brought laughter from the crowd.

"I say, why don't you die, devil? You afraid to die? The longer you stay alive, the more you afraid to die."

"Let's go." I started edging away. When we were clear of the crowd we set off, walking fast, eager to get away from the ugly scene.

The highway leading out of town was in good repair. Vehicles passing were either going the wrong way or were loaded and traveling too fast. Several miles east, we passed a long line of blasted and burned out vehicles. Wermacht bodies were sprawled in ditches partly covered with snow.

Hours later, the road in front dropped out of sight and came into view again a quarter of a mile farther on as it rose out of the valley. We stopped when we identified the jumble of debris bordering both sides of the road where it crossed the lowest part of the valley and stood a moment without a word, then continued. We walked on, our mood in keeping with the shocking remains marking our journey.

When we reached the center of the valley floor, we were overcome, walking on in silence, taking in the carnage – bodies of both sexes and all ages, children and elderly people for the most part. Wagons and contents were smashed, ditches on both sides of the road filled with horses, wagon wheels, splintered wagon bodies, bundles of clothing, trunks, bedding, every conceivable item people might carry with them when they join an exodus in the face of obliterating violence.

Those who had rushed into a new life were now linked in squalor and death with those whose passing had been just as shocking and replete with pain and terror.

Topping the hill on the far side of the valley, we turned and looked back, wondering why it should have such a strong and frightening effect when there was nothing present to harm us.

Teel's voice broke the silence, "We're up shit creek without a paddle – I'm going back, do what you like, I've had it."

The road dropped onto a wide, unbroken plain, its limits obscured by curtains of snow blowing across the hard white surface, hiding fences, roads and burying isolated farm buildings.

Teel's pace had slowed, causing an aggravating stop and go pace that finally brought my warning.

"Unless you want to burrow under a snowdrift tonight, we'd better cover some ground."

"We goofed, I'm going to turn around, go back; the Russians'll gather up people and ship them home. We'll disappear in this used up nowhere."

"Forget it, let's move, let me tell you about a friend of mine who went back…"

"I can't go with another of your fuckin' fairy tales, believe me, enough's enough."

"High school days, a weekend in early October, three of us, close friends, we pack in, plenty of everything for three days, young smart asses, hitchhike to Anacortes, known as 'Annie's corsets', land side of Puget Sound on Fidalgo Island, then ferry through the Straits of San Juan de Fuca…"

"Goddamn, here we go again, places no one else has ever heard of."

Teel had closed up tight, keeping the pace, unaware that I had dropped my voice.

"From Quilcene on the Olympic Peninsula, we hitch to the mouth of the Dosewallops River and turn up into the rain forest, never, never land, Pat, absolutely unreal; blue water below, snow capped Olympic Mountains above, towering Douglas firs covering the slopes, sunshine with a bite in the air. The trees were straight as ship masts, two hundred feet tall, five, six feet in diameter, moss hanging from the branches like drapes thrown there by Paul Bunyan."

"Who the hell's Paul Bunyan? Never mind, I shouldn't have asked, that'd be another story."

"A legendary woodsman, like John Henry, the spike driver, rail layer..."

"C'mon, let's get back to hippity wallopy or wherever the hell you left us."

"Shafts of sunlight came down through the holes in the branches way up above like spotlights on the stage, ground mist moved over the trail whenever the air stirred, kinda' scary."

"Get to it, what about goin' back?"

"Comin' to that."

Teel was so close we bumped shoulders.

"Trails come from both sides joining the one we're on. We take a few detours, can't tell whether they're going to run up a tree, disappear down a badger hole or just get tired and quit."

"Gotta' hand it to you, you've got an insane imagination; get on with it."

"Before going too far, we always return to the Humptulips timber cruiser trail." I turned my head so Teel wouldn't catch my smile.

"Aw, forget it, I'm boring you."

"Goddamn it, go on!"

"Pay close attention, we're comin' to it. We know we're in game country, deer, mountain lion, bear; they come down from the snow country in the fall. Paul Jorgenson begins to sweat about not having rifles and then he's bitching about the grade and he's getting blisters. So, next trail coming up from the left, he stops, you can't see twenty feet at ground level in any direction, but his mind's made up. With the sun almost over the ridge, Paul splits off on a side trail, we go on another half hour, make camp and build a Paul Bunyan fire."

"What the hell kind of fire is that?"

"Bigger than big, giant size. We bang the frying pan against a rock every few minutes, just in case."

I paused, then picked up the pace – Teel lunged to catch up.

"In case of what?"

"Well, he might've changed his mind and tried to come back."

"Did he?"

"No one will ever know, he was never seen again, ever."

Teel walked on for a long interval, then stopped and shouted, "What the hell's the point?"

I looked at him and answered quietly, "Don't really know unless it's 'you can't go back' – that's the way it is."

We walked on in silence, preoccupied as the falling snow became a blizzard.

CHAPTER XIII

Gmezno, Wrzesna, Golina, Konin, Kutno, Piatek, Strykow, a sameness had been stamped on the people. Overrun and overwhelmed by the Nazi juggernaut and long years of occupation followed by Russians sweeping and smashing westward, all of it left a mark, a mixture of suspicion and reticence.

Surprisingly, most of them shared a belief born of a wish that things would be settled soon and everything would be as before.

We sought shelter out of the cities among small farmers and peasants for good reason. In some places the peasants were permitted to remain, produce their crops, raise pigs and supply milk and butter for Hitler's insatiable hordes. Their life style, for the most part, was unchanged although they were allowed to keep only bare necessities for themselves.

They had weatherproof refuge, privacy and extra food hidden at great risk and now there were signs of change giving hope and an answer to their prayers that the war would end and, one day, old ways would return.

Their response to strangers at their door was seemingly without guile or pretension; a nod and gesture ushered them into the warmth, smells and comfort of an all purpose room with an icon or crucifix prominently displayed.

It seemed they possessed an instinct for putting things in their proper places. The wind driving unhindered over the frozen land was bitter cold, one could not sleep outdoors and be alive in the morning. Men traveling at such times stopped because they had reached their limit of endurance, knocking at doors rather than kicking them open, asking quietly and humbly for shelter. In dire need, they stood waiting, speaking in strange, unknown tongues.

We were those kind of men. Our hosts were simple, uncomplicated people who had no voice in their fate, but somehow retained a humane response and seldom turned away those in need.

And there were those who had roomy flats and expensive chattels, tailored clothes and self-assurance, the reward of status and privilege.

Anton Kirski was our first such encounter. From all appearances, he had not suffered the hardship visited on most of his countrymen.

Kutno, mostly undamaged, was jammed with Russian vehicles and sidewalks crowded with Russian soldiers and civilians mingling without any apparent hostility. They haggled with proprietors of shops displaying bakery goods, chickens, vodka, used clothing and boots, all giving off a good feeling, a Saturday night crowd, the kind I remembered in towns at home, not similar in appearance or makeup, but more in laughter, shouts and horns blowing.

"All downhill now, buddy." Teel's smile reflected the robust spirit of the place.

We entered a hotel with an unlit corner sign, a lobby and a raucous bar, working our way to the desk.

"Documente?" The clerk stared as a deep, rumbling voice sounded over the mixture of voices.

I turned to face the source; a Russian Officer, half a head shorter and a foot wider stood at our side.

"Amerikanski, Lager." I pointed to what I thought was a westerly direction.

"Nient documente."

It was a scene repeated on every encounter with military or civilian officials, potential benefactors or whoever pressed for identification.

The square-faced, flat-nosed Russian Major made a vague gesture toward the far side of the lobby. We followed to a table and chairs in a shadowy corner, sat down and were surrounded by Russian soldiers and civilians.

The magic word, 'Amerikanski,' drew a crowd. Three bottles and half a dozen glasses landed on the table. Someone reached over and poured as laughter and shouting drowned out the Major's words. With a trace of a smile, he raised his glass.

We drank and exploded in an outburst of coughing, bringing a roar from the crowd. What followed would only be remembered in bits and pieces clouded by endless rounds of vodka accompanied with plates of ham, cheese and black bread.

The high-spirited hours with our noisy hosts ran a long course until we were eventually bedded down in one of the hotel rooms. We slept until the glaring daylight pouring through large, uncurtained windows combined with clanking tanks and unmuffled engine roars brought us to a painful awakening.

Large, heavy snowflakes were falling straight down, piling evenly on the windowsill, obliterating the building across the street.

For a time I was content to lie still and enjoy the unusual comfort and privacy of our spacious room.

Teel stirred and sat up suddenly. "The grand-daddy of all hangovers – ya' know somethin', the Russians really do have a secret weapon, V O D K A!"

We dressed hurriedly in the frigid room, speculating about the next phase of our journey, hoping Kutno might offer an end to our journey.

Several civilians were seated in the lobby. The parade of military vehicles had dwindled to an occasional Jeep or truck.

A man in a finely tailored heavy wool coat and fur hat approached from the side of the lobby holding out his gloved hand. Except for his apparel, there was nothing unusual about his appearance or manner. Of medium height, he was slightly obese with swarthy skin and common features. He approached from the side of the lobby.

"When I heard there were Americans, I came at once." His English was slightly marred by a deliberate emphasis in the wrong places. "I am Anton Kirski."

I extended my hand, "Jim Hannon, Pat Teel, Lieutenants, United States Army, we were German prisoners."

"And now what are your plans?"

Teel answered, "A quick trip home."

"You come with me, a short walk. We will talk, I can help you."

The snow was still falling, soft and deep underfoot. We followed in single file as Kirski plowed ahead leading us to his home. He said it was two streets from the hotel.

We climbed a flight of polished marble stairs to a wide carpeted corridor displaying paintings and prints on the softly tinted walls, a prelude to the large, luxuriously appointed apartment. Still maintaining his interval, Kirski led us to a parlor crowded with heavy antiques and wall hangings; a blazing fireplace sent out abundant heat.

"So, please remove your coats – sit here by the fire."

He pulled a tasseled cord hanging to one side of the hearth, then selected a pipe from a circular rack, packed it with tobacco, fired it with a sliver of wood held to a flaming log and puffed for a moment while studying his guests. The aromatic tobacco smoke lent just the right amount of coziness to the scene.

"So..." he drew on the pipe, "So..." he exhaled slowly..."Now we shall have some refreshment."

He opened a free standing cupboard, filled three small crystal glasses, handed one to Teel and one to me, then extended his glass with a studied pose. "Salute – United States."

The anisette eased our fading hangovers.

"And to Poland." I offered the response and waited for Kirski to refill the glasses.

He smiled as he poured, assuming a serious manner after our salute to Poland, nodding as he spoke. "After your time as prisoners of the Germans, you are inclined to trust everyone. Let me tell you, we suffered under the Germans, but the Russians, ha! Now we come to something worse, yes, worse I tell you."

He paused to re-light his pipe and then went on. "We did not want Russians here. No, we wait now for American troops to come. We are very close to America, so many of our people in America already. We are afraid because Russians are not like us, not like the Germans, they are barbarians. I tell you what you must do."

An elderly woman entered carrying a tray piled with cheese, sausage and the familiar heavy, dark bread.

"Please, eat now and we will have some Vodka, not that Russian swill, Polish Vodka."

We ate in silence until Kirski leaned back in his chair, re-lit his pipe and continued his unsettling dialogue.

"America and England will soon break with Russia, they will not permit the raping and plundering of western countries. Through the underground we know this to be true. So, now you can help. When you return to America, tell, speak how these uncultured savages are abusing Poland."

He paused for a moment while he assumed a composed, sad, but heroic posture. "We, alone, if necessary, will fight Russians to rid our country of them. We do not like Russians; for centuries they make war on us. Now, when American troops come, you will see Polish people rise up against these invaders. Understand, the German is different, Hitler was a bad man, it is not the German people."

I was uncomfortable, trying not to show it as Teel and I exchanged glances and put down our glasses. There was something wrong with the picture; the apartment, furnishings, a German idolater, long cruel occupation; Kirski didn't give the impression of one who had been abused or endured hardship.

He was standing, pacing, as his voice rose. "You do not know, you in America are insulated from the real world. These barbarians will not leave Poland or Germany and terrible things will be done, worse then Nazis. Thousands and thousands of Polish soldiers have been taken away; five years have passed and none have returned. Remember, most Germans hated Hitler, they could not speak up. Terrible losses in the east because of winter cold, heat and mud in summer and great distance all combined to bleed the German Army to death, otherwise…"

He stopped and stared at me. "You Americans should have seen what fighters they were when they took France." He changed the subject abruptly, sensing he was disturbing his guests.

"Russians have no voice in government, they are not educated, only a select few, not even reading and writing; they live like animals and respect nothing. Not so in Germany, there the people have good homes and education and bring to the world much knowledge, music, art, science and appreciation of family and country. The standards by which we judge men and nations show Russia to be a crude, undeveloped people, intent on enslaving her neighbors and reducing them to the level of the Soviets."

We stood up, reaching for our coats. "We have not seen the things you talk about."

"Everything you have heard about Germans is bad. The Nazis used excessive force, but not all Jews were abused." Kirski straightened his shoulders; there was a challenge in his voice as he spoke with deliberate force.

"I am a witness and a friend of good Jews."

I returned his bold stare. "What did you do?"

His voice was soft but forceful, "I saved the life of a Rabbi and I survived."

"That's what all of us try to do. Thanks for your hospitality."

Anton Kirski was still standing in front of the fireplace, motionless, when we left his apartment.

The sky was bright, reflecting in a blinding glare off a fresh blanket of snow. The cold bite of winter piled on Kirski's revelations made for a heavy load.

We walked in silence until houses gradually gave way to fields and lines of trees extending into a long, descending landscape.

"Kirski, what is he?"

I turned to look back at Kutno; the only identifiable feature was the hotel.

"Polish, a survivor. Let's get movin'."

CHAPTER XIV

In early afternoon we entered Lodz. There were no Russians to be seen. Some of the civilians were well dressed, giving the appearance of people who had known a life of comfort and style before they joined the expendables.

A tall, aristocratic woman spoke to us in English. Her manner was gentle and assured. We accompanied her, a little self-consciously, feeling the stares of people passing by. She walked between us, guiding us around corners as though we needed assistance.

Her actions were kindly, a notable contrast to Anton Kirski. She might have endured great anguish, a common burden wherever the Wermacht had taken command.

During the walk we learned her name was Madame Lubin. Her home had been in Warsaw until shortly after the German occupation when she had come to Lodz with her husband and two daughters where they had been more privileged for a time. They were Jews, she said, or they might have been more fortunate. When she said the word 'German' the intonation was brittle and constrained. We looked curiously at the black walls and gaping windows of a stone church.

Madame Lubin stopped and spoke quietly. "The night the Germans left here we did not know what was about to happen. Often they made arrests for no apparent reason and this night they made many arrests, ordinary people for the most part, individuals and families. There were Jews, of course and many others. Those not arrested stayed in their homes for to go out would be too dangerous. Some hours later, we heard explosions and could see the fire. The next morning the Germans were gone and inside the church were the remains you will see later, buried together, impossible to identify and so, we have another monument to German culture."

She spoke with unmasked bitterness, making no effort to hide her feelings. Several blocks further on we walked slowly past the cemetery, a grave marker showing through the snow.

I felt uneasy. 'Indifferent to death,' a remark I remembered someone saying who had seen too much killing and had become unmoved by the sight of violence. Strange words, perhaps they were used to hide fear coming from being too involved with death.

My view had changed; violated bodies had once brought on a concern and strange repulsion, but that had passed leaving something else; I was not sure just what it was, certainly not indifference. It was more a loathing and a feeling that the masking of man's savagery was a defensive thing born of a need to put it out of sight.

The dead were at rest, not so for the many living. For all the ways they suffered I felt a strong empathy and a fear that many who did know would forget the enduring lesson of war. It was seldom that I thought of those first months, a time of discovery about myself, important to me alone. Those who had not endured a like experience would never understand the tragedy of the living experience.

Our guide stopped in front of a large apartment building. "Not very handsome now, so it is on the inside, but we are grateful. Come in please."

She saw them seated in the ornate sitting room, then excused herself and returned with a bottle. "We manage some things, it is not the best. We drink when we have the occasion."

For a moment, nothing was said, then, looking directly at us, she raised her glass. "To Poland, poor Poland, the one you see now possesses not much to desire, we are sad but not ashamed."

I answered slowly, my voice subdued, "The story of Poland, the suffering and hardship, to lose your home, your friends, members of your own family and to have lost your country, you must have a deep hatred."

Madame Lubin, hands folded in her lap, turned her head to gaze at a family portrait. "It is not possible to express what I feel. The occupation has meant for Polish people not only brutal killings and concentration camps, but all the indignities, those everyday things that must, in time, reduce people to a very real kind of desperation.

"It is right to condemn those who sold themselves for a loaf of bread or for position; no one can defend them, least of all myself. For this contamination, this awful infection, this epidemic, I hold only the German responsible. Our people who turned against us would not have the reason. They are guilty and they will suffer punishment, still,

77

when a man sees his children starving or a woman is witness to her husband or son hanged, some are not as strong as others.

"Days and months and years of hunger, cold and violence are not things to be imagined to understand how we feel. These things you must have lived, it is not possible for people who do not know the experience to feel the same."

Conversation was interrupted by a noise in the hall; a middle-aged man entered, his smile changed the mood that could be felt in the room.

"This is my husband, Lieutenant Hannon and Lieutenant Teel, American Officers, they have been German prisoners."

"Yes, yes, I know…" He spoke excitedly, "…so I heard in town. They told me the Americans came home with you, I hurried."

He sat down. Leaning forward, he spoke again. "We have not seen Americans for many years. And, so, you are going home to America? Lucky boys!"

He asked many questions, wanting to know where we lived and where we had been captured. He told us he was on the town committee, in charge of questioning people who were being picked up. German military were dressing as civilians in an attempt to conceal their identity, and, because they often spoke the Polish language, it was difficult sometimes to trip them up.

He said he would have to return to the headquarters and invited us to accompany him. We shook hands with Madame Lubin, promising to return later for dinner, and departed with her husband.

The wind was cold and piercing. Walking hurriedly, we noticed the cemetery and the shell of the church casting long shadows. Just before reaching the town square, we turned up a side street, entered a building and followed Lubin into a large room. Town people were seated along one wall with several civilians and a Russian Major seated behind a table at the far end of the room.

Lubin identified us. The Russian Officer, his English adequate, shook hands and invited us to share the Vodka.

I studied the Major; he was rugged with a strong face, close-cropped black hair and wide shoulders. The manner in which he fixed his eyes on his subject gave unusual force to his formidable physical assets.

"Documente." His question was abrupt.

"We're American soldiers." Teel pointed to himself and then to me.

Lubin turned to the Major. "Nyet documente, niemcy lager."

I uncovered my bracelet and pushed my left hand across the table. "My name and Army serial number."

Unfastening the bracelet, I held it toward the Major who turned it one way and another, then, handing it back, smiled and raised his glass.

Our fractured conversation punctuated with gestures and shouts overcame language obstacles. Studebaker and 'Villees' received loud praise and much table thumping as the Major roared out his approval. His voice and arm waving slackened off at the name Ford – still, he showed some grudging appreciation.

Turning to face the rear door, he raised his hand. Lubin explained, "We have only a few people to question tonight. They are coming in now. Please, if you will sit here,"

A line of people filed in and were guided single file to the far end of the room, then back until the first was in front of the table. Standing patiently, they moved forward as the guards spoke.

Lubin spoke to the first man in line. He responded, produced a paper, answered several more questions and, at a word from the guard, left the room. The process was repeated. The Russian Major was smoking quietly, watching the procession.

The next man looked no more suspect than any of those who had preceded him. He was mature, tall, reddish blond hair, wearing a loose fitting one-piece coverall. He answered the questions without hesitation, produced a paper that was examined by Lubin and handed back with a nod indicating everything was in order.

Suddenly, the Russian leaped to his feet, committee members and the man who had been questioned turned as he seized the suspect's collar and with one movement tore his garment open to reveal a black tunic showing German Sergeant's stripes and other markings.

Stunned at the dramatic expose, I pushed my chair back. The man's face was beaded with perspiration. Wetting his lips, he looked at the Major and then the men behind the table.

The room was quiet as a church. He stood mute, a tick pulling at the corner of his mouth; the paper dropped to the floor as he motioned futilely with his hands.

The Major spoke in German, a monologue, perhaps an accusation to establish what was to come. It was high drama with the leaden weight of pathos.

They played out the game. The German looked around the room, at me, at Teel, flicked a quick glance at the Major, wet his lips and dropped his eyes while his interrogator riveted him with a hard, boring-in stare, the look was intimidating; he pointed to the paper and pencil on the table.

In the stillness, splitting cracks of frost moving the old structure's timbers had the effect of a strident 'Achtung'.

Exposed and helpless, the German returned the Major's stare. The Russian walked around the table, sat down and waited. Looking at the paper, the German breathed deeply and shook his head.

Tapping a cigarette partially out of a pack, the Major held it toward the prisoner. There was no response. He stood up with aggravating deliberation, stepped back, lit a cigarette, inhaled and glanced around the room.

Once more the Major tried. With an edge to his voice, his words were not in question form – they conveyed an indisputable statement. He spoke at length and gestured toward the guards.

The German underwent a remarkable change. Standing erect, he moved his head from side to side; his gesture had the air of finality.

At a word, two guards stepped forward, seized the Sergeant's arms and turned him toward the door. He braced himself and stopped, his eyes narrowed as he stared at the Major who pushed the pad and pencil across the table.

I wished I hadn't accompanied Lubin to the interrogation. I had no desire to witness the one-sided affair where the final scene had been pre-ordained. The grim show would carry through; the loser must always pay the price and thereby continue the everlasting process. The next time…the next time…always the next time roles would be reversed as they were being reversed. He thought of Father Hogan's words, "Hatred will never be stilled by hatred, it will only be stilled by non-hatred, that is the law eternal." Buddha, 5th Century.

How many centuries had passed since that philosophy had been expounded? How many centuries would yet come to pass before, if ever, mankind would be able to grasp the undeniable truth of those words? I remembered then who I was and the thought startled me. My struggle and despair was borne of long exposure to unreasoning, pragmatic men. I had a feeling that I was strongly allied with people of many races and beliefs. All things were universal, all suffering, all offenses, all solutions, the answer could not be for a few, it must be for all people or it was not for any.

Nothing was changed, man is a fool, he reaches, grabs, achieves, then is gone, forgotten as though he never was, a moment of time, a transient unable to comprehend his significance, the Reich that was to last a thousand years would be gone in ten.

I remembered the bullet splattered and abused cemetery on the Anzio Beachhead holding the revered remains of the hero patriot Garibaldi and the G.I.'s urinating against it, striking matches on convenient protuberances as they exclaimed, "Another bust out Dago."

There was a strong inclination to intercede in the present proceedings, in some way to plead, to find a solution other than the obvious, but I did not interfere.

When the sound of the automatic fire came, I broke into profuse sweating, a feeling of suffocation seizing me. Ignoring the Russian and Lubin, I walked across the room and stepped out into the cold, feeling a great need to be away from the room, the scene, the final moment in the life of a soldier, an enemy, S.S., a man whose lonely, unnoticed passing took something irreplaceable out of a spectator who had a concern too deep to bury.

CHAPTER XV

We entered Warsaw in mid-morning. Bent and shattered remains of what had been tramcars lined the way. Walking casually, we instinctively felt concern – where there should have been traffic there was none.

Gradually, the evidence of a great city began to build up along the road. Buildings were much like they had been in the smaller villages, scarred and abandoned, ripped with small arms fire, particularly around windows and doors. Occasionally, a hole had been blasted in a wall, sometimes several holes and small craters in the road and between buildings.

Scrap and wreckage littered the streets. Lampposts were bent at crazy angles with wire hanging limply from crossbars.

Snow was piled towards the sides of the road; here and there wrecked vehicles lay on the road and sidewalks as well as pieces of weapons and bits of clothing. All of it was on a scale that caused us to move close to a front wall when a splitting explosion a block away scattered dust and debris across the boulevard.

Somewhere ahead and to the right heavy explosions sent dust clouds over the skyline – the ground trembled. A loose piece of stone tumbled from a wall as the rumble faded. Minutes later, another blast froze us in place. We couldn't determine the direction of the bombardment or how far away they were.

Moving down the avenue, the buildings grew taller, the scene of desolation greater.

At intervals a military truck or line of half-tracks passed at high speed throwing up rooster tails of snow and ice. Here and there we saw someone standing in an entrance way or crossing an intersection bundled in shabby wraps with faces turned away, going about their never ending search, finding in anonymity their only defense. It was a pretense that seem to say, 'If I can't see you, you can't see me.'

Teel swore, "Goddamn, this is a ghost town."

Steel tram rails in the middle of the street were twisted upwards. Where there were no walls, piles of stone and framework stood like black skeletons above the rubble.

"Doesn't look like the end of our journey."

"You never can tell, Pat."

Teel shot me a quick, puzzled look followed by a trace of a smile.

Late in the afternoon, we crossed the Vistula River on a wooden roadway laid on ice in the shadow of the destroyed stone bridge.

Joining the traffic, an ever-increasing parade of humanity, we learned there was a refugee camp a few miles beyond Praga, a place called the Polygon, offering food and shelter.

"Want to try it?"

Looking around at the refugees, scarecrows in rag picker's garb, Teel shook his head. "No, I don't want to, but, what the hell, maybe we'll learn something."

The street was wide and muddy. Passersby on the sidewalks stopped and stared at us curiously. As usual, we were soon surrounded. After we identified ourselves, the crowd increased and people were trying to talk all at the same time. We waited for the inevitable person who spoke English.

"He's probably spent time in Pittsburgh or Detroit and, ten to one, he'll be an old guy out of breath and his first question will be, 'Where you boys from, Peetsbourgh?'" Teel spoke with a trace of irritation.

Just then an old fellow pushed his way breathlessly through the crowd. He was well dressed, wearing glasses and a little round hat.

"Mister Kirsch, I heard Americans were here, I come at once." He stopped for breath and then continued, "Where you boys from? Peetsbourgh?"

Teel laughed, "No, not this time, New York."

"Are you going to Polygon?"

Teel looked at him, "What's the Polygon?"

"Polish barracks, now refugee camp."

"Where's the camp?"

"At end of street. There are other buildings, inside very big, five sides, five stories high."

"Okay, thanks."

As we turned to walk away, Kirsch held up his hand. "You come with me, eat, then will be easy to find way again, is close, you will see, one street over, you come, have doughnuts, was baker in Chicago. I know you like doughnuts, everybody in America like doughnuts."

"Doughnuts! That did it, Jim, let's go!"

Kirsch took the lead, talking at random about America and the bakery in Chicago, interjecting a word now and then about the Germans and what they had done to him and his family.

The weather had become mild, turning the road into deep, sticky mud. We followed in single file to a small house, battered like all the others with shell holes in the yard. An outbuilding had been demolished and what remained of a house next door was a pile of black bricks and a chimney. We followed Kirsch to the back entrance and up a flight of outside stairs. He saw to it we wiped the mud from our feet before entering.

As we entered the kitchen, Kirsch called out. In answer, a pretty young girl entered.

"My daughter, Alice, speak no English, too young in America, does not remember."

We spoke to her using her name; she didn't understand a word.

The adjoining room was jammed with furniture. Kirsch placed chairs around the table and opened a large album. "Pictures, my place Propotnia, near Posnan. You see, I return with my family, build this place and flour mill."

The picture showed a handsome stone house with a garden and orchard.

"Why are you living in Rembertov?" At that instant I knew the answer.

"Why living here?" The old man choked. "We call Germans Tedeschi. This happen to everyone. They come one day. I am to leave at once; was prosperous man, good business, many horses, cows, furniture, not to take anything, some things we can carry."

Kirsch spoke to the girl. She placed a cloth and dishes on the table and brought in coffee and doughnuts.

While we were eating and drinking, Kirsch spoke about Chicago and seemed disappointed to learn we knew little about the city. A terrible mistake he had made when he returned to Poland, he wanted to return because he was getting old.

"You stretch American dollars into Polish Zloties, they buy more, make life better for family."

Later, we shook hands and thanked him for his hospitality. I wanted to leave and not have to listen; the recitals had a sameness to them.

Following the main road, after passing a savaged forest, we sighted the Polygon, five sides, an impressive structure from a distance.

The first glimpse proved to be incompatible with reality. It was a teeming warren, infested with used-up humanity, a wretched, offensive monument to living rejects.

Something close to anger built in me. Apart from all the reeking things around me, I was momentarily drained of any feeling but revulsion as I stepped over and around filth and slimy puddles.

A muttering wreck enveloped in layers of foul wrappings squinted up at me, spewing out liquid mutterings as he urinated on my feet.

The young had an old look with no signs of humor or laughter, in the grip, like all the others, of some terribly urgent task, wearing remnants of many different uniforms including cast-off field gray of the Wehrmacht. All of them were a pitiful mix, long past classification.

My harsh judgment upset me, contradicting long held views of the unfortunate as worthy of tolerance and forbearance.

A large, open landing in front of the entrance was filled with men clothed in tattered Russian Army uniforms; I thought they were on their knees. Walking through and around them, I saw they were not kneeling – they had no legs!

Some had fashioned pads of cloth with wooden soles for their stumps, hobbling grotesquely like so many dwarfs from place to place, pitifully emaciated and filthy. The yard between the main buildings held more hundreds of wrecks gathered in the swampy mud, snow, water and excrement. Some coughed incessantly, their sodden garments reeking and soiled, misery so complete they wore discomfort as they did their assorted garments.

I was satiated with misery as unwanted pain and suffering anesthetized my natural response. The endless river of forsaken could, in time, erode its crumbling banks as it flowed inexorably to oblivion.

The stench and animal sounds, from the infectious mix underfoot caused me to recoil. Those filling the unsavory, steaming yard had no one to succor them; self-serving resources were invisible. I had no urge to assist.

It was an unfair and cruel reaction. Still, it was a view that surfaced more often as I became more immersed with the war's dregs of which I was one.

"Are you American?"

I glanced to my side and studied the girl standing on the step just above me. Pretty and smiling, she was wearing a man's battered leather coat, a rough wool skirt, ungainly men's shoes and a bandanna fastened around her hair.

"Yes, I am."

"Have you just arrived?"

"Just now. A friend and myself."

"You were a prisoner of the Germans?"

"I was."

"This is my cousin, Millie, her real name is too difficult for you." She put her arm around the shoulder of a tiny emaciated girl wearing a too large and shabby woolen dress.

I had become accustomed to mismatched garments; too large, too small, too dated, too worn, all of that nonsense cast aside as cover, warmth and availability ruled. Her garments covering anyone else would have been ludicrous and comical; the impression was none of those, she was more than accessories or props.

"I am Rose Bergman, we are Czechs. To some, we are only Jews."

"Jim Hannon, Lieutenant."

"Would you like to come to our room and meet the other girls?"

"If you like."

I followed, calling out now and then as I lost sight of them in the shadows and milling crowds. The place unnerved me, particularly the raw sewage odor saturating the stairwell. Our efforts to reach the third floor were akin to swimming upstream with refugees congested on the stairs, as they were everywhere.

When we reached the fifth level, there were fewer people and the foul air had become less noticeable. We passed through two large doors into an auditorium with a stage at the far end. A group of girls and several uniformed men standing near an open window watched us approach. She introduced me; greetings were polite with the exception of an aloof Italian Officer who ignored the introduction.

"This is our group, what is left, from Czechoslovakia and Rumania, we are going home, hopefully."

"Good luck." I looked at her and wondered.

"And you? You will soon be in America and would not like to think about this awful Europe. You will have your family, your home, everything will be as you left it. We know that going home does not mean the end of our difficulties, only a new phase of our life."

The other girls were looking at me curiously, speaking softly in a strange language.

"They want to know where is your home in America, if you are married and how many children you have. You see, they are not very polite, they all envy you very much and I do too."

She looked at me, a little sad and frightened, like a child, alone, calling up all of her considerable bravery and hope. The only thing that could sustain her was an unquenchable belief that better days awaited.

I felt a strange sense of guilt as I answered, telling her I was from San Francisco, California, married and had no children. When Rose repeated his answers the others laughed and made comments she did not repeat.

It was growing dark and conversation began to falter. When I promised to return later in the evening, a clear, tenor voice, soft and sad, interrupted; the Italian was standing in the light of the window. Everyone was very still as he sang in the way seemingly reserved for Italians.

The fading light was centered where Rose stood, Millie clinging to her side. Others gathered around, it was a Raphaelean scene, timeless, reaching a response in me that had never been broached.

I was conscious of a tightening in my throat, captured by the power of the scene. In the center, radiating strength from which all seemed to draw, Rose held my attention. Composed, she looked at me and smiled. I raised my hand absorbing the force, warm and good, steeped in the yearning of the beholder, taking pleasure from a charismatic presence.

All of the accumulated ugliness, the obscene affronts and the misery were forgotten while I savored the scene, knowing she had endured a corner of hell. I felt humbled as the last light from the western sky gave way to the early winter night.

* * *

The urge to move on was overpowering. Gnawing anxiety would not respond to rational evaluation summed up by knowledge passed on by the Russian Commandant of the local forces – as soon as transportation was available, we would be shipped home.

For some who had lived 'behind the wire' patience was in short supply. Once free from prison, we took strength from each other, side by side, with a distrust of any forced confinement no matter how well intentioned.

Adding to the negative side was the suffocating squalor and animal habits of too many, making an extended stay at the Polygon impossible.

The decision required nothing more than, "Teel, I've had it."

"Thought you'd never get to it."

"We'll scrounge what we can, couple of days, nothing happens, we're gone."

* * *

"I wasn't sure you would come. Our room is at the rear, follow me, some of the boards are missing." She took my hand and guided me across the stage.

In single file we passed through the cluttered backstage and stopped when she spoke to someone unseen. A door opened into a room narrow and high with double tiers of wooden platforms serving as beds. An aisle ran between the platforms with small fat lamps throwing off shimmering, uneven light. Several men were sitting on the edge of the lower platform; they gave no sign when Rose told them I was an American.

She named all of the girls; one came forward, shook hands, and then returned to a shadowy corner.

We chose a place some distance from the others, crawled onto the platform and leaned back against the wall. In response to my questions, she began to speak of her home and her family, gradually unfolding another page of occupation history.

She sat very straight, occasionally turning to her cousin and touching her arm affectionately. Now and then she stopped talking momentarily to regain her composure and apologize for her tears.

"Three years past, we were taken from our homes. Before that, it was not easy. At first, when the Germans came to my country they held back. After they went to war with Russia, we felt the change at once. Our little town is not of importance; our home was quite nice with apple trees, cherry trees and a garden with flowers. You would like it, not like America, but, to me now, no place in the world could be so beautiful.

"They made in our town a Ghetto, two or three hundred Jews, not any more. Our old friends who were not Jews did not speak to us or visit us and we could not leave the Ghetto. Still, we were together and we thought that perhaps for several years we would have to endure that life until one day the war would be over and we could return to the old ways.

"Soon, we began to know what it is to live in constant fear. More and more often the Germans came to the Ghetto to search for clothing, furs and precious things. All our valuables had been exchanged for food, coal or wood. When they found nothing, they took someone from the family, and then the young men were taken for questioning. You see, at first, they were pretending and when they became themselves we knew they meant to destroy us.

"Sometimes they came to our part of the city as though they were crazy men. Often they were drunk and those times, if they picked your house, it was terrible. They would take the people to the street, in front of their door, shoot them and stand over the bodies shouting terrible things. We were not permitted to remove the bodies. Later, they would gather up people and force them to bury the dead.

"It is hard for me to tell you these things that must be told; I am afraid not enough can be told.

"There was no hope. Groups of people were taken away, children, young people and the old ones. Then, for a while, it was only men. Our family was still together. We often said to each other that perhaps

89

because my father was a doctor we would be spared, he might be taken away to work for the Wehrmacht as he was often called on to work for them. In this way, we lived from day to day.

"It seemed they were saving us for something special until the order was put out with our names, only the girls.

"The Ghetto that night was terrible. Those we were to leave behind were broken in heart, believing our fate was certain to be unpleasant and cruel while they, only a few now, would soon be destroyed. They were too old or too young to be of any use to the Germans.

"We had a special dinner; the table looked so nice with cloth and candles, like a birthday. We talked of pleasant things from the past. If you could have heard the conversation, you wouldn't have known such terrible fates were hanging over our heads. After dinner, my Father spoke; my Mother and I knew what he was going to say, only my little brother did not. I looked at him while my Father talked at first of the old days and the good life we had for many years.

"Then came the time when almost overnight our world changed. For a long while he never lost hope, feeling somehow this nightmare would come to an end. But now, in the face of what had happened, so many taken away, there was no chance. He said we had been together always, even through the last terrible years. I would be the first to go, after that, it would be him or my brother or my Mother. Soon, there would be no Jews in our town, we should stay together; he had prepared a drink for us, we would not suffer and in a short time we would be beyond the power of the Germans to hurt us.

"I watched my brother all this time. He had listened and began to cry.

"For my Mother and Father and myself, it seemed the best way."

She stopped for a moment and cried softly. I pulled her close in an effort to comfort her. Her cousin, who did not understand English, cried with her. When Rose recovered, they smoked in silence and then she took up the story again.

"I tried to tell my brother it was the only way. He lowered his head, sobbing, and then I was crying. Soon my Mother and Father were crying too.

"This is not easy for me, but you must not pay any attention if I am distressed when I speak. I am unhappy whether or not I speak, I cannot forget, never will I forget.

"For my brother's sake, we did not keep that pact. Soon, we were saying that perhaps even yet we would survive and someday we would be together again, perhaps it was wrong to stop struggling. But I don't think we believed what we were saying.

"So, the rest of that night is not important to my story. We did not sleep. The next morning the German guard came to the house, took me to the street where I joined the others and we were marched away. I could not look back when they came for me. That moment was the most terrible for me and for my family. It is the picture I see when I think of my Mother and Father, not the times when they were happy, and there were many good times to remember, but not the morning when I last saw them. They were not old, but they looked old that day. I think dying would have been easier for them than to see me taken away. I know it would have been easier for me. From there, the story is one you know or could guess."

Rose put her face close and spoke softly in Polish or Russian, then asked me to come back the next night.

"I know one day, any day or hour, you will be gone, forever. Before you leave, come back – I will be ready for your going, I'm not now. You are the first promise I have known that things will be better, come back."

"I will."

CHAPTER XVI

With the first long shadows of night I moved quietly, following the corridor and stairway and knocking at the inner door.

Rose was in good spirits. She had managed to have a shower earlier that day and had clean clothes and decent shoes for her journey home.

"Today my cousin and I were in Rembertov. We felt almost free with our few Zlotys. I am sure you know what this was for us; there were no guards, and the shops and bazaars! To us, it seemed we must be dreaming. In five years this is the first time we could walk freely, wherever we chose, and buy little things that we fancied. There is not much to buy, but still, for us it was wonderful. People here in the Polygon have been so good to us.

"I saw Russians in the shops and on the streets. Crowds of people gathered around them when they stopped to buy something or if they stopped to look in the windows. People would laugh and try to stand close to them.

"Smiles were not for us. When we spoke, the shopkeepers turned away; one took our money, but we were not welcome. A lady in the street told us Jews were not to leave the Polygon. To be a Jew in Poland is to be apart, unwelcome; it is worse than before.

"I am not ashamed to be a Jew, I am angry to be made aware of it every minute and examined with – yes – with hate. Why do they feel this way? Why do they hate us? What are we to do?

"Sometimes we are very much afraid. Our camp was near Torun. When the Germans were gone and the Russians had not arrived, we were not sure what it was we should do. In several days many had gone from camp, our group went to Torun. We were taunted with the word we thought only the Germans used in a bad way, "Jew – Jew." Young men followed us making ridicule, pointing, shouting, "Jew – Jew." People laughed and some storekeepers shook their heads when we tried to enter. We went back to camp, the Russians arrived and sent us here."

She stared at her hands a long time, her eyes were moist. "The spirit diffused too deeply."

The spirit had no reasonable answer but I tried. "They have been taught to hate you. Before there were Nazis there were other whipping boys; some people need whipping boys, someone lower than themselves on the social ladder.

"Jews, wherever they are, have always been a minority and they don't do very well in this world. Hate the Jews, the Catholics, the Negroes; that's the first step, hatred. This war has taught me something, hate and fear are stronger than love; violence is a way men have to get rid of frustration. I think we will win this war, and then what? Will we learn to love each other?"

I was humbled by the realization that I felt an appreciation and understanding for Rose's problem. The germ of racism was alive in all countries including my own.

"Many people wish to see Hitler's work completed, Rose. If I were a Jew, I would get out of Poland, out of Eastern Europe. Live one day at a time, don't agonize over tomorrow. Whatever it takes, get out – Israel or America, Canada, Australia – just get out!"

She listened intently and then motioned with her hands. "The Russians have not made us feel that we are different. With them it is, I think, simply what you are and what you did during the war. They cannot forgive collaboration with the Germans. If you were a collaborator, it does not matter whether you are Russian, Jew or Pole, all that matters is your place during these years. It is an element of the Polish people who keep alive the distrust and suspicion."

"Rose, I felt for a long time the same as you do now. In my mind there was a right side and wrong side; the dividing lines were clear, the edges sharp, the Allies and the Axis, it was that simple. I think our side is in the right, but now I think there is another side, the human side. The people, innocent and harmless, all of the people who just wanted to live their lives and love their children and have the things that were dear to them, to enjoy small hurts and hates of family and community living. But, this, this has become a savage plague and I don't think there is a cure.

"When there is hunger, terror, death and pain, shocking fear and despair for your loved ones, you don't look for right and wrong sides. The mother in the concentration camp who witnessed her son herded to the gas chamber endured no greater agony than the mother in Frankfurt who, after a bombing, watched stupefied with grief as the flattened, twisted, violated blob of flesh that was her child was uncovered. There are no sides then, no right and wrong for those who face the final agony or lonely death."

I paused, lit a cigarette, exhaled slowly and turned to her. "If you were far removed from this planet, on a star, and had the power to look down and observe all the people on this earth, — white, black, yellow, Gentile, Jew, Mohammedan, American, German, Russian, Japanese — I think they would all look much the same and their way of life would impress you as though they were one people with one purpose. Unfortunately, that's not the way it is; people everywhere are suspicious of what they don't understand and so they follow rather than resist and believe rather than question. They turn their heads so as not to become involved and yet are involved from beginning to end."

Silent for a long while, she brightened. suddenly, "Enough of this talk and our troubles, do you have a sweetheart?" She smiled.

"Long ago, in another world, I have someone."

"I know she is pretty, her clothes beautiful, she is about twenty years maybe?"

"She is."

"How old do you think I am?"

"You should never ask such a question. Somewhere between, let me see…"

"Oh, you can be honest, I know you will be wrong." She laughed.

"Let's say twenty-five." I delighted in saying things that brought on her perplexed expression, then relented, "Seventeen, eighteen…"

"Eighteen. I show more than I had hoped. My cousin, she is not yet seventeen, looks like a little old lady. It is not easy to define, the eyes, I think. Others have a vague, frightened look as though at any moment something terrible will happen to them."

"Where will you go after you reach your home?"

94

"I think of it constantly. Palestine, if they permit me. There, I think, people like myself must have a place where we can do things, where we can work and forget as much as possible these years."

I took her hand and looked earnestly into her eyes. "Don't expect too much, there are many who did not disagree with Hitler's treatment of the Jews."

The door opened with a crash as a huge Russian soldier entered and walked past casually. Shooting a hard look at me, he turned, came back and spoke in Russian.

"He wants to know your nationality." She interpreted.

"Tell him."

They conversed briefly, then she explained, "I told him you were a prisoner of the Germans, that you are now like us, a refugee, trying to get to your country."

The Russian pointed to one of the men at the far end of the room and spoke again to Rose. I recognized the word 'Italian' when she answered. The Russian glanced towards the Italian, scowled and spoke to Rose again.

"He does not think highly of the Italians."

Pointing in succession to others in the room, it was obvious the Russian's opinion wasn't very high of any of them.

"He doesn't like the Hungarians, there were many Hungarian Divisions fighting with the Nazis."

I studied the Russian a little more at ease. He was dressed in a tunic with baggy pants tucked into high felt boots with a sheepskin cap cocked over one eye. Several medals were fastened to his tunic; his left hand was wrapped in a dirty, bloodstained bandage.

He was not a young man, probably thirty-five, a face bony and drawn with strong features. Men who have been too long under fire acquire such a look.

"He has seen much of the war, the medal farthest to the right means he has been five times wounded."

"Ask him how long he has been fighting the Germans?"

She conversed at length with the Russian. He answered her questions with an occasional show of anger.

"He is not to talk about where he has been. He began fighting many years ago during the war with Japanese in Manchuria. Now he is Sergeant. He was a good soldier; now, he is not a good soldier unless he is killing Germans, nothing else matters."

"Where is his home?"

This time the Russian responded without prompting. When he finished, I motioned for him to sit down. He accepted a cigarette and interrupted Rose as she spoke as though the question had touched something he wanted to talk about.

"His home was in Smolensk, does that mean anything to you? He wants to know."

"I know there was fighting there, that most of the city was destroyed."

The Russian spoke with rage. "There was fighting everywhere, many cities were destroyed. That is his answer and he does not think Smolensk means any more to you than many other places. He repeated his home was in Smolensk. When the Russian Army recaptured the city, he went home on leave from the southern front. He had lived there all his life; the city was in such a condition, he found the place where his home had been with great difficulty. His was a large family, six boys and three girls, his mother and father. He alone is alive today. His five brothers were killed early in the war, his mother, father and sisters died in Smolensk. He says it does not matter how they died, there is no way of knowing, but they died at the hands of the Germans. In that pile of rubble and somewhere in one of the mass graves, there is his home. He wants to live long enough to cross the German frontier. The Germans have homes and cities, he would like them to know how he feels.

"He wants you to know it wasn't only the Russian Army that fought, but women and children, as much as a thousand miles on the German side of the front. He saw what happened to guerillas and civilians captured by the Germans. When he thinks of his countrymen he does not like to see the other men in this room living. He does not think they hated Hitler as much as they hated Russians. He is a simple man who believes all men, whatever their country, either fought Hitler or they did not. That is all that matters to him."

A long silence followed underscored by the soft sound of voices at the far end of the room.

The Russian sat on the edge of the platform half-turned toward Rose, leaning forward, elbows on knees, with the cigarette between

96

his fingers sending a thin column of smoke to the ceiling. He stared at a mouse close to the baseboard chewing a crumb.

His words stirred memories; all he had now were memories. The good ones were of his brothers, sisters and his father and mother before the horror. Poor city dwellers working, loving, drinking, what else was there? Occasionally, a festival with much food, music and dancing was a temporary escape, a respite from drudgery that bonds those together who work to provide life's necessities.

Gone forever now, times were seen, as all vanished happiness is, through the magic prism that filtered out the bad and enshrined the good. Gone forever were the hopes, the dreams, the giving and taking, the joy and pain, even the dying had added a part to the whole substance of living.

He dug in his pocket, held out his hand and dropped a fragment of white cheese. The mouse bounced high, scampered past the cheese, stopped, slowly approached the offering and resumed the exclusive business of feeding unaware of the source. Suddenly, the Russian lurched to his feet, mumbled incoherently and dropped his cigarette.

I watched the mouse race to a sanctuary where the baseboard parted. A trace of a smile softened the Russian's face as he turned, made a quick, awkward bow, flicked a salute and was gone.

I moved to the edge of the platform.

"You must go? You are kind to listen, I would like you to come again."

"That's a promise."

"You are leaving soon then?"

"Rose, I can't sit and wait, do you understand?"

She nodded as I got to my feet.

"See you tomorrow."

She smiled and raised her hand.

Later, lying quietly on the bunk next to Teel, I thought of them and their quest for a way of life that had vanished, resting in the dusty corridors of yesterday. Rose lived on hope and love as well as a building hatred for those who had destroyed her family and country.

I wasn't sure of what was to come. Something was taking shape within me, a strange awakening or realization that I was, in so many ways, one of the privileged. When all accounts were added up and tallied I had a large edge. The gap was wide, feelings would change, thanks would give way to resentment and, in turn, to envy and, inevitably, to something else.

Without conviction, I reasoned the world would be better now; wars, abuses too numerous to count, those things that went with them were history, never again.

The last night I was awed at the depth of my feeling for her, the vagary of another dawning gnawed and aggravated me.

As I began to rise, she stirred and spoke softly. "Are you awake?"

I turned to her. "I've been awake."

"What is it?"

I waited a moment before answering. "It's the time of day, before first light, that's when whatever fears I have hit me."

"I'm afraid..." She moved away and spoke in a whisper, "...of parting, to be alone again."

She covered her face with her hands. "Please, take me with you, you can take me with you."

I felt the weight of her loneliness. The gray hint of light at the window caused me to pull her close. The wind was rising and something was banging against the side of the building. I recoiled as the force of her words struck him.

"I can't do that, Rose, I'm leaving this morning."

She moved away, stood up and walked to the far end of the room.

Disturbed and ill at ease, I left the room.

CHAPTER XVII

The train slowed, lessening the draught and cold. I sat across from Teel. Leaning close, I spoke his name repeatedly until he nodded his head.

"Listen to me, listen, any day, any hour we'll be out of this. You have to try like you never thought you could, reach down and pull up that last ounce, think of yourself, forget how it is in New York, wall to wall girls and cocktail time."

Teel smiled and mumbled, "It's all that keeps me goin'."

"You're not listening, you have to grind your teeth. None of us knows how much we have in the tank until we're in a real fight, the main event."

Teel moved his right hand and nodded.

I leaned closer. "When I was a kid, I was fishing alone in Salmon Bay, Puget Sound, Seattle area outside the locks connecting Lake Union and Lake Washington with Puget Sound.

"Most of the Yachts and pleasure boats anchored in the fresh water lakes. I've told you this before…

"I was rowing for the dock, light went fast when the sun dropped behind the Olympics. A Friday night, June, full moon, fun people with the bucks were pouring out of the city, pushing their boats all out to reach their weekend Shangri La. Rowing with my back to shore side, I couldn't see boats until they passed me."

I stopped, wondering if Teel was able to hear. Leaning close, I heard the whisper, "Goddamn it, get on with it."

"Something sent me a signal. I turned and looked, fifty, seventy-five feet away was a ship with a towering super-structure, big as a battleship in the half light, bow waves curling away and bearing down fast. Shouting and waving, all I accomplished was to position myself dead flat across the bow; he didn't slow a knot and he didn't miss. The bow cut halfway through my boat, flipped me under that monster scraping the bottom of the hull, terrified of grinding up in the prop,

99

choking, thrashing and praying. Somehow, I was thrown out of the wash and broke surface not more than ten or fifteen feet behind the stern.

"After blowing and gasping, I turned and struck for the beach; the water was colder than I remembered, but the tide was with me and swells were minimum. Shouting was useless, radios and victrolas blared out 'Happy Days Are Here Again, 'Just a Gigolo' and 'Blue of the Night', Russ Columbo, Gene Austin, Ruth Etting – sure I remember them, I still remember the words."

Teel shook his head and smiled.

"I wanted to sleep, close my eyes for a few seconds, then alarms sounded in my brain and I swam all out until I didn't care anymore, it was easier to float…"

I stopped and sat back – Teel opened his eyes.

"There's more, give me the show stopper."

Sipping a drink, I went on.

"Something in my numbing brain kept nagging me, 'you're almost there', 'you can do it', I kicked and stroked believing it was all over. When I stopped, my feet sank down and touched bottom, half-hysterical, I made the beach and sprawled.

"A thought hit me like a hammer…" I raised my voice, "You can't ever quit, can't ever give up hope, so, buddy, reach down, suck up all you've got in the tank and let's go home."

Teel reached out with his right hand gripping my arm as the train screeched, rattled and jerked to a stop.

After an interminable wait in the marshalling yard, the train crawled into a great, barn-like station shed.

Not yet daylight, the platform was crowded and the wind as usual was bitter cold. Teel gripped my arm, his head hunched down into the collar of his coat. Those who had left the train were filing through a single gate at the far end of the station where several uniformed guards checked papers and tried to collect fares.

We moved through the crush toward the end of the platform. Several doors led into offices, light showing through drawn shades. I hammered on a door; two men, with obvious misgivings, opened the door.

Aware of our identity and Teel's condition, they spread a blanket on a desk close to the stove and helped him up. Sweating profusely, his breathing was labored.

I tried to answer their numerous questions, but the heat of the room and the long night on the train were too much for me, my eyes refused to stay open.

Hours later, I awoke with a start. The taller of the two men made signs that we were to go with him. Teel was sitting up holding a steaming cup in his hand.

"You had a rough night."

"This hot Vodka is guaranteed to cure me."

The tall man introduced himself, said he was Basia. He spoke surprisingly good English and invited us to accompany him to his home. Clean cut and gracious, his openness and easy manner put us at ease until we arrived at a tiny house. There, Basia's wife Olga, to his obvious surprise and mortification scolded and pouted in a subdued voice that was more irritating than if she had shouted her displeasure. The language did not camouflage her rude behavior.

Their home was modestly furnished standing on the outskirts of the city overlooking a long, sloping hill. He followed us outside, apologizing for his wife who continued waving and crying from the doorway. Shrugging, he pointed across the valley toward a large camp starkly outlined in the brilliance of the midday sun.

"Majdank, Maidonek, death factory."

We could see the high wire fence and guard towers spaced at intervals around the perimeter. Rows of one-story sheds and a tall, brick smokestack towered above the place.

I could not define my feelings as I stood looking at the camp. Maidonek, the name, had become familiar, a household word, repeated over and over by Poles and Russians during numerous conversations.

There were many of them. Tremblenki and Auschwitz by sheer size were more compelling and awesome than lesser known places where hundreds or perhaps where ten, two or one had died. I wondered if it might have been easier because there were so many of them.

Maidonek, for me, was a symbol of the horror and torture the Germans had brought to an abused country. I stood for a while transfixed. There was no smoke coming from the tall stack that had poured out a black, stinking cloud for five years, not smoke generated by furnaces adding to life, enabling people to work their land, to weave their clothes or make the essentials that serve the needs of the living.

This had been an oily, black smoke, as black as the hearts of those who had kindled the fire, a combination of searing flame and human flesh. It was not the result of an obscene burst of Nazi temper, far from it; Maidonek had been, in every sense of the word, a factory of death.

I was amazed at the scope of Basia's eloquence and knowledge, somewhat less amazed when I learned he had been a history instructor before the war. European history had been both his profession and his religion.

"When the wind blew from Majdank," Basia said, "you had to close the windows, the stench of death would not permit you to breathe. At those times, you could not eat nor could you go on with your daily routine.

"Wind, mostly from the east, drove the black smoke billowing out of the tall stack straight at us; it lay down on every surface a horrid residue and became a constant reminder.

"You could not accommodate it, no one could. Under such a condition people became afraid, a heavy stench of death hung over our heads, contaminating our clothes, our bodies and our lives.

"We called the furnaces 'devil stoves', the camp was the 'death factory.' Poles will never forget the 'devil's stoves' reminding us every minute how uncertain and wretched life had become under the 'master race,' bringing hell to Lublin, to Poland, wherever they set down their ugly regime and created a hell for those who rightfully lived there.

"In fact, they wanted the Poles to breathe and know the smell of death. Fear breeds obedience.

"Everyone saw the long trains bringing the condemned to Majdank. The smell of death from the camp rattled the window panes; death followed you through the streets and into the forests; it smothered Poland."

He described the 'death factory' in detail. "That place over there…" pointing, his eyes grew hard, "…twenty-five square kilometers, prison yards, gas chambers, crematoria, ditches for shooting prisoners, gallows for hanging them and brothels for the guards with a continuing replenishment and assortment of women.

"All told, six separate, identical layouts with an open area in the center for executions.

"The straight paths, bordered by carefully trimmed lawns, flower beds and birch lounging chairs, set the German Administration buildings apart. They lived well. It seemed the oppressive stench of death was acceptable to them. Their gardens grew the finest vegetables in the whole area. Enormous cabbages, sold to certain merchants, were described as tasty and tender, but you cannot eat them and you cannot look at them; they were grown in blood and ashes.

"It was an enterprise which you cannot imagine, and yet, it existed. Everything there, from quarantine to crematorium, was planned and operated to annihilate people, a creation of the military quartermaster medical research and industrial engineers, engineered by compass and slide rule, discussed and planned as if it were to become an important commercial project.

"The camp remains as it was; gas chambers, crematories, barracks, storage sheds, gallows, barbed wire enclosures, searchlights and dog runs. The dogs remain there still, German Shepherds. They look up quietly from their kennels, perhaps bored with their idleness since they now have no one to catch and ravage. The ovens and terrible stench remain as well as tables for butchering the half-burned skeletons.

"There are here in Lublin, those who were prisoners and witnesses who escaped the slaughter. They say, 'I lived through it and cannot understand why I am alive, I saw it and cannot comprehend how I remain sane.'"

Basia pointed across the valley. "Never forget Maidonek." He turned, facing me, and pressed a small book into my hands. "Oboz W Majdanku, Maidonek, take this home – your word may not be believed. Here is the story, Maidonek, hide it in your coat."

And there it was, two kilometers across the valley bordering on the Lublin-Chelm Highway; the guard towers, wire fences, German buildings reflecting the bright light of the living world. Above all, towering and ominous, the great smokestack like a giant enduring tombstone marking the finale to that obscene drama.

"Believe in angels..."

Teel turned his head and stared at me, his look was puzzled as though he had not heard or understood my remark.

"The devil's more like it."

We could make out the road on the far slope winding up to the camp, becoming obscure in the fusion of bright sun and glaring rooftops covered with snow.

It was easy to see the long lines of people. Jews, patriots, saboteurs – non-Germans, that was enough and those whose age had spelled their doom, the young and the old.

What must have been their feelings as they walked through the gates into something that had earned a reputation so awful that many, on learning where they had been sent after being unloaded from the trains, simply froze in place. Nothing the Germans did would influence them to walk another step; they died in the shadow of the 'death factory'.

Most had walked through the gate hoping that somehow they would be spared, that someday they would leave the camp, and they did, 'up the chimney' as the 'gallows humor' had it.

Walking down the slope after thanking Basia, we glanced back; he was waving, seemingly immune to his wife's hard thrusts echoing off the hill in the clear, still space around them.

All prisons impart a grim, sobering threat; Maidonek held us with a quiet horror.

I had stood on ground where people had died. This was not a moment of reverence. The horror and scope of what took place washed over me; I felt hot and breathless, skin on fire, scalp itching as I stood at the gate where the hordes of condemned abandoned all hope and gave themselves over to what was to come.

What desperate thoughts assaulted them, some stoical and calm, many hysterical with fear and shock, all would have suspected what was waiting for them inside. The German guards, cloned by the astonishing new order, would have been in character, shouting and clubbing those who did not move fast enough. More likely they clubbed and abused to keep themselves occupied and demonstrate their conscientious devotion to the their duty.

The gate was open and unguarded. We walked inside, paused and looked around. A civilian and a Russian Officer approached from the guardhouse just inside the gate.

The Russian spoke first, appearing puzzled when we did not understand. Then the civilian, and again we shook our heads.

I interrupted with the single word, "Amerikanski" and pointed to Teel and myself. The civilian smiled as he answered in our language. He spelled out his name, Steven Niemwiez. I said we would like to know what had happened behind the wire. The Officer and Niemwiez huddled together; finally, the Russian shrugged his shoulders, glancing curiously toward us.

"He will permit it. He said our visit was not uncommon, come with me please, here it is left as it was, still echoing with their cries. I was here every day, I still see them."

The long sheds stretching out along the walkway served the inmates as shelter until their turn came. For the days left to them it might have been that a numbing worry dulled the impact of mundane things. Many died during the interval, before the shower ended their lingering agony. The deliberate and unmasked manner of the killing would have been unimaginable for so many, yet it may have been preferable than to die from starvation and exposure.

Closer to the incinerators, another building had been divided into five large bins. As the line of condemned passed by in one bin they left wallets and jewelry, in the next their shoes then their coats, pants or dresses, underclothes and so on until the last where they left their hair.

We stood for a time contemplating the pile of shoes – high heeled, ladies button shoes, all sorts and sizes – children's shoes, pathetic little ones with one or two buttons. In the next bin their coats, then pants or dresses, underclothes and so on until the last one where they were shorn of their hair.

We walked into the tightly sealed shower room, without windows; overhead pipes and showerheads looked real enough.

Niemwiez said the prisoners had been jammed in indiscriminately until the room was filled, then the doors had been closed and barred. A guard turned a valve and minutes later the door was opened, blowers cleaned out the fumes and future victims removed the pile of contorted bodies to the next operation in line. The shower room was ready for another group.

The crematorium was so situated that it could be kept in operation by any one of the several gas chambers without lengthening the haul. Piles of ashes and bones were stacked around the cold furnaces and some in the firebox.

Teel stood quietly, shaking his head. "What is there to say?"

I thought of those who had died there and wondered if the people of America realized how near the shadow of the smokestack came to our shores!

We passed row after row of wooden barracks and worn footpaths. Those entombed had known they were to die in a day or several days, a week, a month, what did it matter? The fact of their death, at that point, was established beyond their power to alter or prevent. What would they have talked about – the weather? Who would be next? Their state of health? Rumors would have been born, circulated and laid to rest while the latest was already establishing or destroying the credibility of its predecessor.

I sent Teel a look. We shook hands with the smiling Niemwiez and the indifferent Russian, turned and walked toward the darkening sky.

Near the bottom of the hill, we turned and looked back. The sun behind Maidonek silhouetted the guard towers and the towering smokestack. Rising wind moved the dry surface snow in swirling sheets through the looming 'death factory', sending up to the heavens a haunting, wailing sound that might have been the despairing cries of nine hundred thousand murdered victims.

Night came with surprising suddenness on that ravaged land bringing on concern as the wind sounded continuous warnings, sweeping loose snow off the crusty remnants of the winter blizzards.

"There's a light…" Teel shouted as a blinking, yellowish point showed and vanished just off ground level. "O.K., let's go for it, it's close to the road."

"That's our target for tonight."

The farmer seemed concerned as he led us to a stall, spread a generous layer of hay and then, from the shadows, carried folded horse blankets and dropped them on the hay.

Communication, as usual, was a combination of arm and body language interspersed with vocal supplements in English and Polish; we were to stay in the barn, he would bring food, we could spend the night and move out after daylight.

The plan went off without a hitch. Bread spread with lard, a generous chunk of cheese, and a hot drink of something resembling coffee.

Other than for the usual animal noises, we were undisturbed as fatigue, warmth and food put Maidonek out of our minds.

The pervading quiet made more private by the stirring of animals brought on an unusual sense of well being and the memory of her that grew stronger with each passing day.

Time was too short, made more precious knowing each day and each hour would be relived over and over in the months or years that would measure time lost away from her.

CHAPTER XVIII

San Francisco, where Ginger and I met, came alive, little things weighed heavy. Evenings often beginning with dinner in places picked at random, a stop at a sidewalk florist where I'd buy a corsage, usually a fragrant gardenia and then the few hours that followed.

The circumstances of massive military forces in Fort Benning, Georgia made living accommodations for most something best described as primitive. The gracious home where we were married and lived would always be remembered for the unforgettable pleasures we shared those months before the inevitable separation.

Pulling the blanket close, I held on to the memories and the blessing of our meeting and gave a silent prayer of gratification knowing there would come a time when the forced separation would finally end. I fell asleep holding on to her, to the exclusion of all other forces past and present.

Light crisscrossed the stall from outside as we awakened to sounds of the animals and the farmer's greetings.

"Another day, it might be better not knowing what's to come."

"Knock it off, Jim, maybe we can talk him out of something for the road."

While we were brushing the hay and chaff out of our hair, the farmer pushed aside the hanging harness. He smiled as he held out large loaf.

"For you, take, soon now we have no war, all like before."

Teel took the bread. As I tried to thank him our host pulled the harness off the rack and turned away.

"Thanks…" I smiled as I shook my head.

Teel's short fuse was easily ignited. Sameness and uncertainty was a heavy load, adding fuel to his smoldering anger.

"That dumb son-of-a-bitch really believes when the war's over everything goes back to normal. Cows are givin' milk, hay's in the meadow, sun's shinin' and the bad guys are all dead or in jail. Twice in his stupid life he's been run over by a steamroller and he still thinks it's all a bad dream, shit."

Glancing at Teel, I patted my stomach and seemed to be talking to someone invisible as I sighed. "A full belly can change your point of view."

Teel mumbled something unintelligible.

"You know, buddy, you may be a little hard on the good farmer. People are sometimes too quick to pass judgment. Somebody said, think it was Jesus, 'Judge not less ye be judged'."

Teel moved closer and half shouted, "I can feel it comin', another of those made up stories that happened to you way back that's goin' to explain that stupid Pollack."

"Matter of fact, when you were cuttin' him up, something that happened to me the year before I left St. Paul's popped into my mind. Believe it was May or June, we were always scheming, trying to figure out a way to make a buck or two bits; money was harder to come by than a kind word. Someone said it was berry picking time in Puyallup Valley, that wasn't too far away, twenty, thirty miles."

Teel interrupted with a curse, "Son-of-a-bitch, didn't anything ever happen to you in a place a normal guy can pronounce – like Smithville or Brown's Corners?"

"I left after breakfast, got lucky, an old fellow picked me up on Fourth and drove me all the way. Stopped at a sign beside a gate with a 'Pickers Wanted' sign. Lots of people were already out in the rows of huckleberry vines, mostly women, girls and young kids. The farmer gave me a flat, a box with twelve small berry boxes in it, and a strap so you could hang it around your neck and pick with both hands. He put me in a row all by myself. I looked around; a woman here, a kid there walked out of the rows, handed their flats to a woman, probably the farmer's wife, she made a check on a tally sheet, gave them another flat and they went back to the row."

I laughed, "Looked pretty good to me. I didn't know how much the pay was, but even the little kids were turning in full flats, so I went to work."

I was quiet so long Teel broke the silence, "Come on, I know that isn't the end of the story, no way."

"Well, in one way it is, in another it's only the beginning, I'll shorten it up. By four o'clock I hadn't filled one flat and the others had picked four and five, one little guy had picked seven. I watched him, his hands flew. Seemed I had a bad row, had to search for every huckleberry, pick it, put it in the flat. Anyhow, four o'clock the man blew a whistle and everybody came out of the rows, I was close to the head of the line. The man looked at me, then at the berries, finally, he shouted."

"What the hell are you doin' here? A blind man could do better than that."

"Then a cold-eyed, skinny harpy behind me stepped up and shook her finger at me, 'Know what I think, Mister Evans, I think he's the one who robbed the tents and I'll bet that's what he's been doin' today.'

"Well, a lot of others got in the act, I was up a creek without a paddle until Mrs. Evans said, just in time, 'I'll call Fred Sanders, he dropped him off this morning, come with me, son.'

"Sanders told her he had picked me up at Fourth Avenue in Seattle before nine o'clock that morning. When we were alone, Mrs. Evans gave me a dollar and walked to the road with me. A good woman, saved me from those huckleberry pluckers."

After a lengthy silence, Teel let go again, "O.K., what the hell's the punch line?"

I looked at him for a moment, laughed and stopped. We stood facing each other as he shook his head.

"Like I said, judge not, you never know the story behind the other man's act. Two years later I took a Coast Guard physical – so help me, I'm red-green color blind, a bad case. You know, buddy, those bitches would've hung me and my only crime was that I couldn't see those huckleberries, green leaves and red berries were all the same to me."

CHAPTER XIX

Epaulets showed his rank, equivalent to Captain in U.S. grading. Chapka and long cloth coat were well kept accenting his slender body. Taller than most and decidedly more threatening, he fastened on to us in the skeleton of the Radom railroad station.

I smelled trouble from the moment I turned and saw the intense stare boring in from the hard-eyed, scarred faced Captain.

"Ignore him, keep walking."

"It won't work, here he comes."

A frenzied civilian carrying the usual packhorse load of bundles and boxes chose that moment to stop and adjust his baggage blocking the way.

"Documente."

It was never a request, always a challenge, carrying with it an aggravating insinuation that you were up to your ass in crocodiles.

"Here we go again." Teel whispered.

In a louder voice my response was as close as I dared to mimic the Russian.

"Nyet documente, Kreigsgefangener, lager, Americanski Offizier."

"Kamerad – Kamerad." The Russian raised his hands in mock surrender. His voice and expression came across as a contemptuous put down. He turned his head shouting something unintelligible that sucked three soldiers out of the crowd beside the first coach.

"Amerikanski nyet soldat."

"Screw you." Teel's remark, fortunately, was wasted as was my admonition.

"Goddamn it, take it easy, this is a mean son-of-a-bitch. I'll try another line."

"Russky dobra soldat." I smiled, nodding my head vigorously.

It didn't work. Pistol in hand, the Russian waved it in the general direction of the patched up offices beyond the last coach. The inscrutable enforcers stuck their rifles into our backs. I moved and Teel followed, his earthy language unrestrained as the rifle hit a nerve.

The room smelled of urine and a gagging mix of other unidentifiable matter, bare of furniture other than a long stand-up desk against the wall.

A Polish ancient wearing a battered peaked cap and coat with a brass button here and there labored with his new commission as interpreter.

"Who you?" He seemed lacking in any enthusiasm for the job.

"Amerikanski Offizier." I pointed at Teel and myself.

A torrent of angry language from the Russian recklessly waving a 7.5 millimeter automatic equipped with a notorious hair trigger set Teel off again.

Leaning back and away from the pistol, he shouted at the Pole, "Tell the son-of-a-bitch to holster that goddamn pistol!"

A flood of Russian sent the unhappy interpreter reeling. Just then a non-com stuck his head in the door. His shout and arm waving sent the Captain flying toward the train. When he disappeared in the crowd, we moved fast and ran toward the opposite end of the train.

The station was the usual pushing and shouting bedlam. We learned by means of our improving universal language that a train would leave in a few minutes for Jaroslaw; the journey would require several days since the track was under constant bombardment.

Coaches were swarming with people loaded down with sacks and bundles. Several Russian and Polish Officers were standing near a coach at the rear of the train.

"That must be our Pullman."

"Broken windows, no doors, I don't see a diner."

"Those Russkies are all packing their bags. I haven't seen one yet who didn't have a loaf of bread, a slab of bacon and a bottle of Vodka tucked away somewhere. I think the guard at the gate and those other people are nuts. According to our map, Jaroslaw is not that far from Lublin, my guess is four or five hours."

Teel's eyes were bloodshot and his face was flushed.

"I hope you're right."

We stood apart from the others until the whistle sounded, then chose a battered compartment at the end of the coach and sat down as the train started up with a jolt. The track veered off from the marshalling yard sharply to the left and soon we were rolling through the outskirts. Houses, stables and trees were blanketed under heavy snow and the bitter wind was blowing a fine white powder through the smashed windows.

We moved to the inside of the compartment away from the windows in an attempt to escape the force of the wind as speed increased and the cold crept up through our legs. We went silent as conditions worsened and hunger pangs added to our misery.

"I'm feeling bad." Teel coughed and shivered; his eyes were watery and his face was a livid, hot to the touch.

"First stop, we unload, find a house and stay put until you're okay."

"Jaroslaw maybe, but not before then. That's a pretty big place, the way I feel now I may need help. Let's keep goin'."

"The way you feel now you better last to Jaroslaw; you're right, you are going to need help."

Standing up I danced around between the two long wooden seats, stamping my feet and flailing my arms, then walked to the window staring at the bleak, lifeless picture as the coach bucked and rocked. Tiny houses with scattered trees, flat, white fields and wreckage alongside the track had a sameness and look of desolation altogether, a sack of stones on my back.

Teel was motionless, giving no sign that he was aware of our building crisis. I stepped out of the compartment into the corridor, walking, stomping and jogging in place trying to drive the aching cold out of my feet as the wind tore through the coach. Glancing into other compartments I was amazed to see Russian and Polish Officers were not paying the slightest attention to the cold, shouting above the racket and smoking as though they were riding in a heated Pullman.

I stood there, face close to the shattered glass, until they turned and faced me. One of the Russian Officers got to his feet and walked toward me.

"Panamya Russitsch?"

"Nyet panamya Russitsch, panamya Anglish."

The shoulder tabs identified the Russian as a Colonel. "Yes, understand English." There was hardly a trace of an accent.

I was too surprised for a moment to respond.

"What are you doing? Where are you going?"

"Home, the long way around, wherever and whenever we find transportation. We were prisoners, an Oflag west of Warsaw. My friend is sick, he's in the next compartment, if you could spare a little Vodka?"

The Colonel stared for a moment then slowly began to smile, "Of course, I have Vodka." Picking up a cloth sack he said, "Will you go first, please?"

Teel looked up for a moment as we approached, then slumped back into the corner.

"Take a good pull on this bottle. The Colonel says a pint of this and you're good for thirty below – come on, take your medicine."

Sitting up gradually, Teel reached for the bottle and took a long drink.

"Hey, take it easy…" I eased the bottle out of his grasp and turned to the Russian.

"Do you mind?" Without waiting for an answer, I swallowed, coughed and swallowed again. I drank again before handing the bottle to the Colonel.

He said nothing, and then his smile gave him away. "What kind of English is this?"

"American, please sit down."

Conversation flowed easily as we drank and ate white bacon fat and dark bread. I forgot I was cold or had been ravenous.

Without thinking, I asked, "Why didn't you take Warsaw last August when the Poles attacked the Germans?"

A long silence followed. The Colonel pulled the cork from the bottle, drank slowly, held the bottle toward me, speaking quietly while he stared at the white blur outside the window.

"You are a student of military strategy?"

Unprepared for the question, I stammered. "Not exactly, we expected, that is, in prison we followed your blitz from Smolensk to Praga and thought…" Sipping the Vodka, I shrugged and waited.

"Do you know our armies had traveled four hundred kilometers without regrouping? Many strongly held pockets were bypassed during the continuous advance; supply lines had been stretched to the limit and more. The Vistula was our objective, nothing more until supplies, replacements, men and equipment and fuel could be moved up. The group of armies in the center, Marshall Rogossovski's armies, one of three army groups, all had outrun their supplies. The Northern group, the Central group and the Crimean group, three army groups extending twelve hundred kilometers across the front, in total, more than two hundred and fifty divisions. Can you comprehend moving, under fire, in contact with a strong enemy, two hundred and fifty divisions and supplying such a force four hundred kilometers across enemy held territory?"

Without waiting for a response, he leaned forward. "In addition to the problems of organization and supply, the next move had to be planned and coordinated, crossing a formidable, natural barrier, the Vistula, with enemy troops, panzers and artillery, dug in and waiting before all preparations had been made would have been a blunder. All of this should have been known to the Polish Commander. Rogossovski is not a fool, good Commanders wait for the moment that will insure victory; a frozen Vistula would not make a problem, a flowing Vistula forced a good commander to wait. When the attack was resumed in January, all preparations had been made, the Germans were routed."

He reached for the bottle, leaned back and relaxed. "Brave Polish people died in an attack that was premature and, from a military standpoint, foolish. We did not duplicate their mistake. Perhaps there are people who would have us make a blunder, allies are brought together for selfish purposes, for survival, for convenience, to buy time, not because they are friends."

He leaned back and closed his eyes while I attempted to respond, a little overwhelmed by the numbers. My question, under the circumstances, had been provocative though it was not meant to be.

I shook Teel to a state of consciousness and saw to it he ate some of the bacon fat before he sank deeper into a troubled sleep. I mentioned my concern.

"He should not be traveling. When we reach Jaroslaw, put him in hospital, is something you must do."

The Colonel picked up his sack and placed the bottle on the seat. "Have a good journey."

"Thank you, Colonel."

There were endless lines of blasted and burned railroad cars and locomotives beside the track. Fields were showing patches of snow and long, clear stretches, deep trenches followed the edge of the forests. Here and there inert green bundles sprawled where they had fallen.

Hours later, the train slowed, clanged and jerked to a stop then lurched into motion. We were crossing a wide river. A timbered bridge had been built on the steel bridge the Germans had dropped into the water, the middle span landing upright on the river bottom; ten or fifteen feet of steel work protruded above the ice.

A huge station shed was a replica of the Radom Terminal, proving to be typically confusing. In the darkness we lost sight of the Colonel and worked through the crowd to the street.

Russian soldiers were everywhere, singing and shouting, many of them drunk, walking arm in arm, passing bottles from one to the other. I noted the civilians avoided the crowded sidewalks and guided Teel to the street.

Several times Russians stopped us. Although I knew we were being questioned, I made no attempt to answer. Shots were cracking in the frosty air and occasionally bursts of automatic fire. Teel moved docilely as though he was walking in his sleep.

Two soldiers in Polish uniforms stepped off the sidewalk and barred our way. They were young and nervous, speaking rapidly and gesturing wildly. I made an effort to establish our identity and tried to explain that Teel was very ill; they turned away and motioned for us to follow.

Near the center of town, one of the men in the lead disappeared into a narrow alleyway. After a moment, he emerged and led us into a shadowy café. Sitting down, we waited while he carried out a long conversation with an old lady wearing a shabby robe. She glanced casually toward me as I studied the two soldiers. Their tailored uniforms and black polished boots didn't fit; their manner disturbed me. When the conversation came to an end the Poles removed their great coats and hats and took places across the table.

"My name is Jan," said the taller man, "and my friend is Franck. We are Officers, Lieutenants. I speak English, good. You have been prisoners, I understand, you not know who Poles despise..." He leaned across the table and his friend moved closer.

"...These barbarians, these Russians..."

He smiled as I shot him a blank look.

A little ruffled, he continued, "German is cruel, but cultured. Not German but Nazi who did terrible thing. Russian is beast, stupid, he is, how you say, envy how we live in Poland. Not go home until we drive him out!"

He laughed, "We can fight. I think..." he stopped for a moment, "...America not like Russians, you will help us." He looked at me eagerly.

"Everybody can fight."

"Some Communists and Jews still, not as many as before."

"Of course. What did you do before the war?" I looked towards Teel who was stretched out on a bench asleep.

"We had land, much land in Silesia. I studied England, France. Now, we have nothing, new government says all will be divided, taken from us, given to peasants."

"Do people want a new government?"

"Most are simple people, they take and say nothing. Some know what to do."

"Jews and Communists?"

"We did not have Jews on our land, Communism is only for those who have nothing, they make equals of all. These Russians, these drunken Mongols and myself equals?"

"Hardly." I looked directly at Jan.

"German and Polish are much the same, can you compare these Russian Officers and German Officers?" He laughed arrogantly.

"Are Germans good soldiers?"

"Ah, Germans are soldiers, all the world knows this. German Wehrmacht, magnificent."

"And the Russians?"

"Rabble. Bah! Soldiers, Officers, drunken peasants."

"This drunken mob of peasants, as you say, seem to be winning."

"Terrible winters, mud, they are not soldiers."

I sipped from the glass of Vodka the woman had placed close to my hand.

"Maidonek, do you know what it is?"

Jan waved his hand impatiently as he leaned over the table and answered. "Work of Nazis, they do things in passion of war, all armies do. There are people, Polish people, who do not want Communists and Jews here; Communists take away our freedom,

Jews take our money and banks and factories, they are slaves of the international Jewish bankers."

I was tired, weary, would it never end?

"Do most Poles feel as you do?"

Jan nodded vigorously. "Of course, there are still some Jews and Communists, not as many as before."

I shook my head and stared at my glass. "No, not as many as before."

Leaning back in my chair, I tried again, "Where's your home?"

He ignored the question, apparently disappointed with my response.

"When the war is finished, America will occupy Germany and Poland, they must push the Russians beyond the Bug River. You will find good allies here, arms only are needed. German troops will surprise you, they are good soldiers. Together we will clear out rabble, you must tell your government."

"One day you'll have everything you want, only trouble is there won't be anyone left to do the work. Good people will have to mine the coal, plow the field, clean the shit house and milk the cows."

We looked at each other, then Jan apologized, "I'm sorry."

He stood a little unsteadily and buttoned his coat; seemed stunned as he motioned to Franck.

"Excuse me, please." He left the room.

Later, weary and a little confused, I noticed the woman was gone. Jan had spoken to her and she had insisted we stay the night. We stood awkwardly for a moment not knowing what to do until the woman returned and motioned us to beds in the adjoining room.

Teel's voice was little more than a whisper, "The unflappable Jim Hannon is slippin' out of control."

Lying in the dark, the street sounds diminished. Traveling down half remembered trails lined with fading faces I made an effort, such as it was, to think through and pull out of the past some common sense answer to our dilemma.

"We're tumbleweeds, going where the wind takes us, trying to follow an unmarked road. We're classic undiluted bums, not contributing to the fight, not helping anyone and, worse, not helping ourselves. Nothing's changed.

"Away back, really wasn't that long ago. Grabbed a freight in the Portland yard, target, Reno, Nevada. It seemed like a place I might find what I was looking for."

"Hey, buddy, didn't realize you were that far gone, you're talking in your sleep."

I turned on my side. "You sound better – I was thinking out loud, looking for an answer."

Teel sat up, his voice a little angry. "I beat you to it; along the way you talked me outta' goin' back, you were wrong. Don't misunderstand, I'm not as smart as you, but I know when things are going against me. No more bullshit." He waved his hand over his head as I responded.

"O.K., you're three times seven. One thing for sure, I don't have anyone to blame, every decision that got me here I made."

The inky darkness was dissolving; lines and shapes were pushing out of the shadows.

Teel was turning and talking. "Take it easy, I've been confused since I started to think, if you have a plan, lay it on me."

"You're worried because you don't know where you're going and you're not too sure I do. It doesn't really matter as long as we keep moving."

He reached out and grabbed at me. "What the hell do you mean 'it doesn't matter', isn't that why we're putting up with all this shit? Tryin' to get somewhere?"

I sat up, "All depends on how you look at it. Reminds me of something an old hobo said to me one day in the jungle alongside the Portland freight yard..."

This time, Teel didn't miss, he had a firm grip on my arm.

"Seriously, tell me you make up these stories, admit it, then go ahead, I'll listen, you've got a captured audience."

"Does it matter? They're all real, we've all heard stories and had experiences, maybe they stay with me longer. Anyhow, the old timer was sitting close by the jungle fire – do you know what a jungle is? A hobo jungle?"

"Yeah, yeah, where they swap lies and cook up a stew, everybody puts in somethin'."

"Well, I asked him where he was going; he looked at me like I was stupid, rolled a cigarette, and looked at me again before he answered, 'I blow around, anywhere to anywhether, ahead of snowballs and behind bakin' sun, travel light and don't make friends, free as a Canadian goose. Owe no son-of-a-bitch a red cent, sleep under a tree or on a pile of sacks, work when it suits me and walk when the wailin' whistle calls. If'n the good Lord's willin', one morning I won't wake up, I'll be with all the good people who steal your house when you miss a payment and the bastards who pays you on Saturday half what he said on Monday when he had to get the boxcars loaded or pay demurrage; with the bulls who hustle you back down to skid row so the thieves who spend six days robbin' the poor can exercise their righteous manners on Sunday and don't want to haf' to look at the victims. So, if'n you'll spear those two tatters right there in front of you, give me the big one, the small one's yers.'

"He put the hot potato in his pocket, stood up, winked at me and headed, whistling, to a just made up freight with no engine or caboose – he didn't know whether it was going east or west."

I smiled and went on, "Which way? We don't have options, we'll get there whenever and wherever."

"You know something Jim? I'd like to've known you before. A West Virginia coal town didn't have much, but to me it was the world, the whole world until I went to New York just before I was drafted. Tell me, what's next? I know there's a message."

"Stay away from situations that spell trouble and do all we can to stay alive, a day at a time."

I regretted the decision that had terminated my life with the Jesuits where I would have absorbed a good measure of useful knowledge and, under constant coaching, developed an orderly mental process. They would have opened the way to disciplined thinking, not the random, spur of the moment reactions that were plaguing me now.

The precise moment the change began was the first day out of the lager. There it was, the main street in Schubin, the blazing eyes of a gaunt German in the long line of prisoners filing past. That haunting stare found me, singled me out among all the bystanders, civilians and Russian tankers, boring straight in, penetrating my conscience, marking my crossing into a twilight zone where all passing things were more personal in meaning. I was leaving behind a dimming and obscure world that would have rejected out of hand my building impatience with the war's pitiful rejects.

I was conscious of my evolving intolerance of most things and people, formed as I was being formed by the massive weight of our circumstance.

"Where've you been?"

I looked around the room then answered as I stood up, "Replaying the past, how about you?"

"I'm stayin' alive for what's to come."

"Let's go find it."

CHAPTER XX

The curious stares and smiles had become commonplace. Occasionally, we would stop long enough to point ahead and ask, "Pryzsmsl?" When the passerby nodded his head, we went on.

Teel had fought his way back, the fever had abated; he was less vigorous but alert, showing more interest than he had for days. At a roadside stall I paid two hundred zloties for a bottle of milk. As we walked I urged Teel to swallow a little at a time and set a pace we could maintain.

On the outskirts of a town we overtook a parked Ford truck piled high with oil drums and sacks of grain. Four Russians emerged from a house close by; they looked at us and took their places atop the cargo.

I approached the driver, identified myself in the usual manner and pronounced the name of the city as I had been taught the night before. The fellow shook his head. I repeated the request, stressing the fact that we were American Officers. The man answered at length, then, realizing he was not understood, stepped out of the truck and pointed to the truck's springs, they were pressed flat. Nodding, we walked away. A hundred yards farther on the truck overtook us, slowed and stopped. All four Russians shouted and motioned us to climb aboard.

All day we passed broken villages with little to distinguish one from the other. In late afternoon when the wind increased I urged Teel to lie down. The others changed their positions and placed themselves to shelter him.

Teel smiled and whispered, "Pick up on the hobo story."

Leaning close, I reminisced about my early years on the road.

"Sometimes, back then, I felt like a leaf dropped off an Elm Tree, caught up in one of those blustery Indian Summer winds going wherever the force directs. I traveled around trying to keep ahead of the frost and out of the hot sun, which keeps you from putting down roots. Of course, you don't accumulate much in the way of chattels and movables, but, like the man said, 'Ya can't have everything'.

"Back then, a hundred years ago, in never, never land, that's what it seems like now." I swallowed a drink and handed the bottle to Teel.

Just then, the truck stopped on the outskirts of a city. The driver shouted, "Pryzsmsl", pointing ahead.

As we walked in silence, weariness, darkness and cold eroded our earlier optimism. Near the center of the city we were directed to the office of Mayor Stanislaus, a great bear of a man, genial, gracious, full of sympathy, coming off as genuine and full hearted. We exchanged views of the war, and then the Mayor explained the views of the Polish people. When our fatigue became obvious, he stood up and placed his huge hands on my shoulders.

"Those who wanted to be German, they shall be. You will wait downstairs, please, I will have a man take you where you will stay."

He shook hands with each of us, walking with his arms across our shoulders.

"Well, so, Americans..." He turned back to his desk, still smiling and sat down. "Your war is finished."

We waited until a young civilian approached. He stood close to Teel, said something in Polish and walked toward the door.

"I guess that means me, Jim, see you later. Make this our meeting place."

"So long, be careful."

Teel stood uncertainly, then turned as another young civilian entered the hall and walked directly toward me.

"Amerikanski." He grinned and stared.

"Okay, that's me."

"Ho kay, ho kay," he laughed. Walking beside me he told everyone we passed that I was an American Officer.

Climbing a long hill, we finally turned into an apartment house entrance that was incompatible with the surroundings, a reminder of home.

I studied the combination of glass and steel, polished marble, long rectangles of glass blocks and the setting of the stairway as the guide squinted at the directory, then led the way up one flight and halfway down the corridor. When the door opened, the man inside bowed and stepped aside.

"Please, come." He spoke as though not sure of his words and led the way through the hall into a room shadowy in candlelight with impressive leather furniture.

"Please, sit."

Tall and thin with dark hair and sharp features, the man's eyes were steady and piercing, at odds with his uncertain manner and humble posture. The empty left shirtsleeve was cut off and sewn together a few inches below the shoulder.

I held out my hand. "Hannon, Jim Hannon, you are kind to take me in."

"Please, I am happy to do. Doctor Boguslaw Halikowski, good to have you, I have many questions. I have no occasion to speak English for many years, as I talk, it comes. You are Officer in American Army?"

"Lieutenant, I don't mind questions."

They came, one after the other. In his eagerness he sometimes forgot to wait for an answer, then appeared embarrassed and smiled. How is it Germany could fight so long? When would it end? How was it the English and Americans had been so long at the Rhine?

I tried to point out the Americans were also fighting a big war in the Pacific. Nodding as though he had not thought of that, the Doctor brushed it aside, asking the same questions in other ways, not comprehending Germany's strength. They had believed Poland alone would stop the Wehrmacht and could not understand the collapse of the Polish Army. They waited then for England and France to make a quick end of the war, almost six years had passed. Russia and America had joined the fight and Germany was still resisting.

My answer was if they had realized the strength of Germany they would not have expected such miracles and added it was a mistake to refer to the war with Germany alone on one side and the Allies on the other.

The true situation was different. America and England were not prepared for war. Germany had all the resources and labor of Europe, the near East and Africa.

"Don't question why it is taking so long, be thankful it is almost finished."

Halikowski lit a cigarette. "We were not to know, only that Germany was winning. It was good Russia stood against Nazis. After invasion of Russia, I went to Tarnopol, a German hospital, wounded came straight from front, not like German before. Something happened, to recover meant to be sent again to Russia, soldiers not march and sing like before. If German soldier unruly, Officer would say, 'Would you like go to Russian front?' It was enough. The cold, Russian guerilla, Russian Army grow in soldier's mind. You could see surprise, not sure now about victory. Herrenvolk learn fear, many not believe victory in Russia. Not trust new leaders. On other side, Russians believe in victory. One became weak, other grows strong.

"Here in hospital, work is too much, too many patients, more waiting. Typhus epidemic, no serum, few drugs, medicines poor quality. Many hours, day and night, we help with what we have, I am doctor. Money? Few have money.

"Old way is gone. I believe all must work together, all people, Jew, Gentile, Catholic. I do not say well in English what I think."

He rummaged through a pile of papers on his desk.

"Here, German friend, nineteen and forty-one, he writes, 'The lack of soap is hard, lack of fuel is here already, you need special allowance from Police before you are allowed to buy shoes, but allowance is never given. Terror is systematical, so successful; I think it impossible anyone living under normal conditions can realize, can think what it feels like. Many people abroad do not like to know, better to shut your ears. And when you go on and on telling them, they look at you and think you are exaggerating, it can't be as bad as that. Nineteen thirty-two peace loving Germans began to warn western people to be aware of Hitler, they did not believe it. It was like that when first refugees went over to the west, they did not believe them.

"If the western powers opened their ears and minds more quickly this war could perhaps have been avoided. It is the same now. The terror in Germany has, so far, been complete success for government. People are executed in great numbers, shot, hanged, innocent people taken from their beds. There is never a trial, they disappear and, if their people dare to ask what became of them, they have same fate. Outstanding people and people with bank accounts are in great danger.

"What you feel about Nazis is known, the size of your Nazi flag, expression on your face, your going to church, your maid is questioned always, books you read, choice of friends, reason for journeys; how hard you try to avoid traps, these things give you away.

"People in beginning of war still dared to protest; they are dead or silent now. A very dangerous moment has come. People have suffered so much they stay in their home, they are afraid to read, to write, to travel, to listen to radio, to go to church. They have lost all things and all freedoms. They have only one chance, to betray others, to be Nazi. The only other thing is to suffer everything, to hope nothing, to try nothing.

"From where will help come to end it? We cannot end it, nothing will break the power of the Nazi government. Call us cowards, fools, oxen, beasts of burden, whatever you like, but realize from this side no hope exists.'"

The Doctor lowered the paper and sat still for a moment.

"Would you mind reading all of it?"

"Some is not about Germans, this page, here it comes again, 'and from where will a revolution come? It is foolish to think Germans will make an end to the government of a lunatic. The officer wants to go to war, the Nazis are his career; if Hitler disappears the job of officer will be unnecessary, so get on with it. Better do the wrong than lose good life. The young boys will fight, they are trained in a most skillful way and will be excellent fighters because to be less they will come under suspicion.

'They are much more safe in Army, even at front, because the cannon you know; the spy at home you never see, the bullet from behind will not miss.'"

He stopped suddenly and stood up. "Excuse, please, something to eat and drink."

I stretched and yawned, tired but stimulated by the missionary zeal of the Doctor who came through as a troubled, disillusioned, used-up professional.

Halikowski pushed in a cart with dark bread, sausage and a coffeepot making me sit up and wonder when the mysterious provider would appear.

Occasionally, it appeared the Doctor thought to hold a cigarette or do something of long habit with his left hand, and then he would look at me uncertainly and, with haste, complete the task with his right hand. He did not act as of he was accustomed yet to the loss of his arm.

"No time to think, when not working in hospital, sleeping."

For the first time he showed a deep emotion, not looking directly at me. "I made many Germans to recover, to go again to Russia to kill more Russians. A contradiction there, sentiment with Russian, hate for German. They could not help themselves, I could, I did.

"Shut your eyes to things, do not fight Nazis, then, you are some way not so much victim. Money, position influence me little. Among us is this, I think, find man or woman who would not go to America, Canada, Australia, that would be surprise for me.

"I think I will go somewhere, our country is dying, cannot survive more struggle. All our lives we work, now we are tired."

Someone called to the Doctor from outside the room; he stood up at once. "My wife, she is impatient. Dinner waits, I must hurry to hospital. Please."

He stood aside, insisting I go first; there was a trace of a bow.

I stopped when I saw her; she was small, well formed and strikingly beautiful. Carrying the smallest child in her arms, she moved quickly between the stove and table.

"Prasha." She looked steadily at me and pointed to a place at the table. The Doctor talked throughout dinner; his wife's cool indifference found its mark, I was fast losing interest in the conversation.

I felt the Doctor was paying too little attention to his family. His wife displayed no interest in her husband's attempts to draw her into the conversation.

When she left the table with the children I relaxed and smoked a cigarette while the Doctor plied me with more questions and insisted that I stay to rest and become strong enough for the remainder of my journey.

He excused himself saying that he must go to the hospital, insisting that I remain seated at the table, Madame Halikowski would soon return and would be disappointed not to find me there. I knew it would be awkward to be alone in the apartment with her.

"Prasha." She was standing very close. I stood up quickly and faced her. Looking at me intently, she turned away and signaled me to follow.

The room was spacious, furnished with quality chairs and glass cases lined with rows of instruments reflecting a feeble candlelight. A long leather table filled the center of the room. I turned full circle, unsure of myself.

While I was standing uncertainly she entered, arms piled high with pillows and blankets. Smiling and speaking in Polish, she broke the tension while she spread the blankets on the table.

"You speak English?" I thought I might have misjudged her during dinner. Shaking her head, she walked out of the room and closed the door.

I undressed, blew out the candle and crawled up on the hard table. The privacy and stillness of the room brought on a sudden urge to close my eyes.

I stirred uneasily, not knowing where I was. Half awake, I had tossed and turned in the grip of some wild, vague dream, I was conscious of a presence and sat up. Things began to take shape in the feeble light filtering in the narrow window from the moon far down on the horizon.

She was standing close, her beautiful face serene and calm, her perfume sweet and compelling. There was an ethereal quality about her. It may have been the result of the waning moonlight in consort with her fair skin and white garment. She stood close, unmoving. As my eyes became adjusted, I could make out details; she was wearing a single garment, low-cut, sheer and clinging to the contours of her body.

In much the same manner as she appeared she was gone, quickly and silently; I reached out to one side and the other, then settled into an uneasy, restless sleep.

CHAPTER XXI

I made my way out of the building and walked quickly to the mayor's office. Someone shouted behind me near the street entrance.

"Raus, maken schnell!" Teel laughed uproariously. Red-eyed and reeling, his eyes were pinpoints of fire.

"You look awful. Where are your quarters?"

Following Teel's garbled directions, I found the apartment house and led him to bed. When he began to snore I glanced into the hall, staring incredulously at an R.A.F. uniform. The Officer was short, erect, dark and hawk-faced. He appraised me coldly; though he was inches shorter, he imparted the feeling that he was looking down.

"You are also American? The Leftenant's friend?" He accentuated the words American and friend. I didn't answer at once; his displeasure was obvious.

"We were German prisoners, escaped and have been on the road too long. Your uniform looks good, someone from the other side of the world, I respect the English, they fought alone waiting for us to give them what they didn't have."

I waited, matching the Officer's stare. "You don't approve of our being over here?"

"I don't approve of people like the one in there."

"The one in there gave what he had."

"Many have given all they had."

A long silence followed, then he introduced himself.

"I am Squadron Leader La Borce." He spoke as though he was issuing a command. "I am from Prague."

"Lieutenant Hannon."

"Come in and sit down." La Borce led the way into the living room; a casual manner replaced his revulsion.

With a wave of his hand, he said, "This is my apartment." Without waiting for a reply, he went on, "I was trained by the R.A.F. with others of my country. Some of us, fortunately, still live and so, now that a portion of our country is free of Nazis, we will be returned to our homeland to continue the fight."

He relaxed momentarily, accepted a cigarette and made no attempt to conceal his pleasure as he savored the tobacco.

"Your friend was escorted here yesterday as you know. He drinks too much and talks too loud." His tone implied he did not harbor any respect for Teel.

"But, he is my friend." My quiet words found their mark. "I have no feeling for those who couldn't have survived without our help and now put us down as soldiers."

"I'm sorry, I am perhaps too critical. The Americans in England were too often the same." He indicated the bedroom with a motion of his head.

"I must tell you it was a great disappointment to me to discover these things about Americans. Their shocking manners, their atrocious way with money; is it a characteristic of your people to be so reckless with money?" An expression of arrogance marred his strong face as he held his chin forward.

"It could be, many people at home think we give too freely." It was meant as a put down, thinking of the equipment, clothing, food, money and lives that had enabled the British to stay in the war. One attitude with money didn't seem much different than another since memory is unarguably short lived.

La Borce's chin came down, his expression softened as my words penetrated.

"I think you may be right about the drinking and loudness." I paused and took a light on my cigarette from the cigarette La Borce held out.

"It seems Americans drink to get drunk! Like it or not, that's the way it is." I had no wish to continue the thinly veiled sparring match; there were more important questions.

"We would like to get on. Are you familiar with the road to Czechoslovakia?"

La Borce took some time to answer. Methodically, he rose, stepped to a small chest of drawers, opened one and, after a search, returned.

"I advise you to report to the Russian Commandant of this city and let him decide how you will be returned to your forces."

I didn't respond.

La Borce continued, "Here is a map, please look closely. You will follow this road through these named towns to Dukla, which lies against the mountains. From there the road goes over the mountains by way of Dukla Pass. I cannot tell you what you will find on that journey, it has been reported there are many bandits and elements of German troops living in the forests."

He inhaled casually and continued, "The front is to the west. It is close, not more than a few kilometers. After Dukla, there are few people until you reach the border. It is our understanding the border is heavily patrolled and where the pass goes through the road it is barricaded. Russian guards permit no one to pass unless they are citizens, Polish or Czech. Across the border is the first city of importance, Metzilaborce. Then, here, eighty kilometers more, is the present capital of my homeland, Dynow.

"Dynow is a city little damaged. There will be many people there, important people. I think when you reach it your journey, or the worst of it, will be over. It may be possible by aircraft to be transported to Moscow or Italy or even London; I think this may be done."

He stopped momentarily. "After you pass through Dukla, there will be few people; there may not be any. Dukla Pass was the scene of much fighting. There may be small groups of houses, nothing more, much has been destroyed."

My questions were being answered before they were asked. The Squadron Leader was as well informed about the next phase of our journey as anyone we were likely to meet. He accepted the fact that I was determined to go on and did not attempt to change my mind.

"Is there an aircraft here that might give us a lift?"

"Absolutely not."

I thanked him for his time and information and, a little apologetically, for the hospitality he had extended Teel. My remarks were ignored.

"You will need money. We do not have an abundance, but for just such things as this we have some. You will find a need for Polish money and Czech also, if you get that far." The hard edge had returned to his voice with a hint of sarcasm.

"We'll make it." I answered confidently.

We were standing. La Borce looked up and stared long into my eyes.

"Do not make a show of bravery with me," he said slowly, "I think you are foolhardy. Here are five thousand Zlodies and two thousand Kronen. I do not give you as many Kronen for two reasons: first, we do not want to finance Nazis and I think they have a better chance of spending this money than you; second, if you are fortunate enough to reach Dynow, you will be provided for by others." He turned as if to leave the room.

"Perhaps I can return the favor for someone else."

I was grateful, but felt a need to terminate the conversation. La Borce made me feel like an adventurer embarking on a lark while other men still had fighting and dying to do.

He looked back over his shoulder. "You can do something for someone else, there is an American citizen here who will certainly not see her homeland again. It is unlikely she will ever see another countryman unless it be yourself." He hesitated and again imparted the impression of looking down from a greater height.

"Of course, what can I do? Where?" I stammered awkwardly. The unexpected reference to another American, a lady, young or old, took me off guard.

"If your friend will remain where he is, I will take you to her. She is here, in this building."

He led the way to the next landing and pointed to a door at the far end of the hall. "In there, Miss Agnes Lloyd."

I extended my hand but the Czech had turned quickly and was gone. In a way I was relieved to see him go.

Thinking more of the Squadron Leader than Agnes Lloyd, I knocked lightly on the door.

"Come in, please."

It was a sunny voice with the fragile quality of many years. Still, it did not prepare me for Agnes Lloyd; an ancient small face looked out from a mountain of pillows and quilted bed covers.

"What is it? Do you want something of me?"

There was a small trace of a brogue and an inflection of culture. Her room was bright and clean with two large windows on one side of her four-poster bed. I entered the room and stepped close to the bed. She showed no concern; her eyes were brighter, that was all.

"Miss Lloyd, I am U.S. Army Lieutenant Jim Hannon." I waited a moment and added, "I'm passing through Pryzsmsl on my way home, if all goes well."

She stared, smiling, as tears formed. I moved closer. With a barely perceptible motion of her hand she indicated a chair beside the bed.

"You are an American soldier? How do you come here? Are there more of you? Please tell me." She reached for my hand.

"I am an American soldier, Miss Lloyd, I was with our forces in Italy. I have been a prisoner of the Germans now trying to make my way east to Hungary, Rumania or wherever I can contact American Airmen."

She studied my face intently, increasing the pressure on my hand.

"God bless you."

There was no attempt to conceal the emotion in her voice as the tears fell unhindered. Her control and dignity were intact and her voice was surprisingly strong.

"It was, for many years, my constant prayer that I would be permitted to return home. That was long ago – for some years I have known it would not happen."

She was composed; I could detect no sign of despair.

"You will return home, Miss Lloyd, and soon. The war is almost over; even now, the way is open to Moscow and many eastern cities." I was groping but there was nothing I could promise.

I didn't think about her age other than to know she was far advanced in years. There was something else – her position, the room and her attire told me she did not leave the bed. My remark to the effect that she would soon return home did not seem to impress her.

"I think for you to come here is enough, a visitation..." she was still holding my hand. "...I have been in this room for three years. Many years ago a family from here came to America for a visit, the Paluski family. They had several small children and I was retained as tutor and companion. They were Jews, gentle people who prevailed upon me to return to Poland and continue my role. It was pleasant and I became one of the family." She wiped her eyes.

"The estate is not far from here; it was magnificent. I became afflicted in later life, a paralysis. There was nothing left undone that might have helped me; specialists in Vienna and Berlin were of no use. But life was still beautiful, not a day passed that the little ones, grown men and women now, with their families, not a day passed without a visit and flowers and gifts. There was talk of sending me to America; I spoke of my home more often and reminisced, but I was not unhappy here." She stopped and closed her eyes before going on.

"The Germans came and our world ended. The family told me nothing, but I could see the change come over them all at once. Laughter and happiness vanished, nothing was the same. Everyone stayed in the great house or, at most, did not leave the grounds. There was a blight on our lives, faces became older, no longer children in my eyes." I nodded and waited.

"One day the girls came to my room; it was a long time before they could talk. German soldiers had driven to the house without warning; when they departed the men were gone, forever!

"The Mother died soon after and we all died a little each day after her death. There was no need to tell me that soon the girls and children would be gone. I lost my will to live. When the Germans came again for the girls and children I pleaded with them to take me too or end my life."

That wouldn't be like the Germans, I thought. Easing pain was not their way of doing business.

"Miss Lloyd, your story, these things happened wherever there were Germans. I know how it must be with you; still, we must go on and live if only to tell others. The western world has a cross to bear, we may carry it for a long time."

"Lieutenant Hannon, that is the right name, is it not? The fate of my family, and they were truly my family, was such that there could be no happiness for me in America or anywhere.

"When they carried me to this room, I had some money and things of value. Most things they took, but not everything, and so, I lived here. When there was nothing left, I lived not much differently than before; you see, others have been good to me. A Russian Officer was in this room one day. By messenger, he sent me money and food. The flyer, have you met him?"

I nodded as she continued.

"A good man, visits me often and yet, I have not seen him smile. He promised when the Americans arrived he would send the first one to see me. The Germans destroyed my world, but this has not kindled in me a hatred, my sorrow is for all people. I think it is not right for

134

anyone to hate as La Borce hates. His view of Germans and his desire to destroy them will consume him. However hatred is engendered, it destroys all other feeling and finally the person himself."

She paused briefly and then asked, "Are you alone?" Is there no one with you?"

"I have a friend, he was also a prisoner. He is with others. Miss Lloyd, we would like to carry a message or messages for you, is there anyone in America?"

"I think not. It has been too long, and then, to what purpose? I will not be living when you reach your home. I know this, it is a feeling I have."

I felt it too and thought it strange that the thought was not reflected in some show of sadness.

"My friend and I will leave Pryzsmsl today, we're impatient – that comes from having been a prisoner. We must go on."

She looked at me for a moment, then squeezed my hand. "Of course, you must, I understand."

With two of the La Borce bills in hand, I leaned over the bed and kissed her lightly. She did not seem to notice when I placed the money on her pillow.

"Goodbye, Miss Lloyd, I'll never forget you."

I turned when I reached the door; she was crying and holding out her hand with the money.

"I do not need this, please, you must not leave this."

"Goodbye." That was all. I walked quickly to the apartment on the floor below hoping Teel had left something in a bottle.

She had kindled an overwhelming desire for an end to the journey and its never ending cast of abused people.

CHAPTER XXII

We made our way across the river on the girders of a bombed bridge and turned south. The ruins of a suburban business district were visible. Our destination had its entrance at the bottom of a half-flight of stairs in the corner of a battered three-story structure; there was a heavy drape across the entrance. Teel held it to one side, then followed me inside.

For a moment, the darkness was impenetrable. Finally, with the help of a number of flickering candles, shapes rose out of the gloom; a cabaret type place with tables and chairs encircling an open area. To the left, an alcove tunneled under the street was Teel's immediate goal. Light from candles exposed R.A.F. uniforms and garrison caps.

The Flying Officers were friendly, exchanging the usual trivia that accompanies first drinks, Vodka, straight as usual.

They refused to let us pay. The drinks went to work at once bringing a feeling of elation so unusual I wanted it to last. The tallest and grimmest of the three officers seemed amused at our antics and attempts at humor but did not enter into our happy state. Occasionally, he would ask a question.

"Where in America do you live, Leftenant?"

I spoke of a small community near San Francisco but that if ever I returned, anyplace in California would do.

Repeating 'San Francisco' and 'California' as though he liked the sound, the flyer sighed and shook his head. A short time later he put the same question to Teel and when Teel answered New York, the Officer repeated the name several times, staring at his glass and, again, shaking his head.

After a while, he asked about Florida, Texas, New Orleans and many other places. Always his reaction was the same, so much in earnest and depressed or angry.

We spoke to the other officers and later Teel mentioned the tall Officer's sadness in an attempt to lighten his mood.

The Officer leaned forward, staring at us; with an oath, he dashed his glass to the floor. Still holding our drinks, we faced him and waited.

"I amuse you." He moved his arms violently, his attitude threatening.

Putting down our glasses, we faced him. In a rage, he shouted furiously. "Do you know what I'm going back to? Nothing, nothing at all; not California, New York, Florida, I'm going back to a town with one well in the square for everyone, not one piece of plumbing, no electric lights, six of us. And all of that was before, how do you think it will be now after the Nazis have smashed everything they didn't steal?

"You can say, 'why go there?' Why? Because a wife and children are there, five years ago, and not one word. They may be dead, may not be, they may be gone, but I will go there and wait because they will have no one else."

He turned back to the bar, "Does that amuse you?"

We had seen little to amuse us; we had no answer.

This time, my money was acceptable. The Flying Officer emptied his glass before taking it from his lips. Soon after, we were good friends again, but not like before. We talked around things that upset him to no avail; he ended every discussion with expressions of anger. Although it was apparent why, it became a burden we didn't need.

On the far side, near the tables, three musicians, with a mandolin, violin and accordion played a gypsy ballad on a raised platform. It was sad; it seems gypsy music is always sad. I thought the whole world was sad and I was getting drunk.

We moved to a table beside the floor. Several couples were dancing; the women had looked better from a distance. They were not young; their clothes were shabby and ill fitting. They pressed close to their companions, young Polish Officers, in the throes of discovering romance

Watching the performance of a couple close to our table, the woman appeared shocked when the Officer leaned far over, whispering in her ear. She cast a frightened look around the floor, then, with abandon, pressed closer against her partner.

Oran, Algiers, Naples, Pryzsmsl, I wondered why whores in public places always tried to act like schoolteachers. We were silent until the music stopped for an intermission and the floor cleared after an interval of frantic caresses.

Idly surveying the patrons, my gaze settled on a lone Russian Captain occupying a table once removed from us on the edge of the dance floor engaged in the universal diversion of getting drunk.

Despite the closeness of the atmosphere, he had not removed his sheepskin tunic or his heavy chapka. He was a hard-faced man with the kind of face that alternated between quick, generous smiles and fierce scowls. During intervals he became intent and reserved. His facial expressions reflected his appraisal as he slowly observed the other groups.

A waiter approached his table, placed a setting of bowls and cutlery, then stepped closer with his pad and pencil.

Turning his head slowly, the Russian stared at the waiter. Suddenly, with a single motion, he sent everything on the table crashing to the floor. The waiter, frozen in place, pad and pencil still poised, sent the Officer into a fit of unrestrained laughter, slapping the table with one grimy hand and then the other.

He had become the point of interest although he seemed unaware as he searched under his chair for a moment, then placed a heavy cloth bag on the table. One hand disappeared inside the bag; with a flourish, he held aloft a long pointed blade and a fork. Again, the hand disappeared into the bag, another search and then, aloft over his head, a large chunk of gray cheese. We exchanged looks with the tall Czech flyer who joined us awaiting the next move.

In turn, with the same deliberate search and air of expectancy, he withdrew a piece of white hog fat, a battered loaf of bread and, finally, a gallon demi-john. Gravely and slowly, he stood up; the room was very quiet. He was a notable presence in the tight fitting sheepskin coat with a full skirt capped with his fierce countenance and once white sheepskin chapka.

We straightened in our chairs and moved our feet back expectantly. The Russian covered the distance to our table in two strides. With one swing of his arm, the jug left his table and landed on ours with a crash that should have splintered the glass.

"Karasha tovarich." He was grinning.

"Same to you." Teel was on his feet and I followed; the Czech pilot remained seated. When Teel told the Russian Captain that they were Americans, he said "Da, da," as though he had known all along. Filling the three glasses, he took a long drink from the jug.

"Nient soldats." He waved his arm to include the entire assemblage.

We understood his meaning, but were not ready to sever relations with the rest of the world. He remained standing, insisting we drink. He filled our glasses and returned to his table.

Teel made a sound like air escaping slowly from a punctured tire. The Czech arose and, without a word, departed.

Meanwhile, the Russian devoured the cheese, the white hog fat and the bread, interspersed with swallows from the jug. When he had consumed his meal, he carefully repacked his bag, all but the Vodka, took off his chapka, laid it on the table, placed the bag under the table, then draped his coat over a chair.

The musicians were playing again. The Officers were with the same ladies who were a little more inebriated, more coy and risqué. They were swaying unsteadily in the center of the floor.

The Captain reached into his bag and withdrew a long handled, elaborately designed mirror. Holding it at arm's length above his head, he studied his left profile, his right and looked into the glass from different angles. Despite the fact that his hair was cut short, while appraising himself in the mirror he ran his hand over his head several times arranging his hair. Opening his mouth wide, he examined his teeth, upper and lower. When he looked toward us again, Teel indicated in pantomime he was curious to know about the mirror. Holding the mirror over his shoulder, he made several vicious chopping strokes with the heavy edge. "Niemcy," he said, patting the mirror and nodding his head.

Sometime later, when the dancers left the floor for places more suited to their needs, we noticed the Russian digging in his bag again. This time he drew out a long, white lace ladies' glove, raised it one way and another for all to see, held it against his face and shut his eyes as though reliving some ecstatic moment. Finally, he drew the glove over his hand – it would not go over his fingers, the top of the glove reached almost to his elbow.

He shouted to the musicians who broke into a gypsy air at once, as though they had been watching and expecting the command. Moving his chair, he stood up, the glove in place, right hand resting on his left shoulder and danced, circling with his eyes closed. Occasionally, the white lace glove would touch his face, eyes or ear and stroke his hair. His expression became more eager and intent as the hand moved over his face.

After a long performance, he reluctantly removed the glove, carefully put it away, then, with the bag in one hand and the jug in the other, placed the jug in front of me, touched Teel's shoulder, smiled and walked away.

Hours later, we stood up and made our way to the exit detouring around the tables and pushing through the curtain onto the deserted street.

The impact of the cold and silence in contrast to the noise and foul air of the cellar brought us awake, aware of our drunkenness. Slipping and stumbling down the steep bank of the river, we walked unerringly to the twisted mass of steel over the water. Teel said he had managed the crossing twice the previous night. A smashing blow to my back put me on a girder ten feet below; the sharp pain in my back would become permanent. Miraculously, we reached the far side.

The door to the Squadron Leader's apartment was unlocked; we entered and managed to reach the sleeping room without incident. Teel collapsed on the mattress; I pulled off his shoes and jacket, covered him with all available blankets, closed the door and hurried to the Halikowski apartment.

* * *

The sky was changing, a tenuous line drawn between night and day, more darkness than light when my worst fears weighed heavily.

My urge to move on was assailed with the rumbling out of the west. A hand drawn map given to me by Squadron Leader La Borce would take us close to the battle line before we turned east toward Dukla.

A combination of loneliness and fear rising out of alarming stories of marauding Wehrmacht bandits eroded my early confidence. Piled on top of time lost behind the wire and hoping the ugly madness would burn out, I closed my eyes. Finally, pushing aside all negatives, I whispered, "There are no options, keep moving, get out of this graveyard."

The smell of coffee and sound of children's voices pulled me to my feet. I dressed, repacked my bindle and opened the door. Madame Halikowski stopped close enough to touch.

"Good morning, Sophia."

She looked one way and the other, then a cry from the kitchen. "Prasha." She brushed past me and hurried along the narrow corridor.

Sophia's attitude was more aloof than the evening before, indicating I was to take my place at the table. She changed noticeably when I declined with thanks and told her it was imperative I find my friend at once.

Notwithstanding her manner, I was moved with pity for her. She did not insist I stay nor did she accompany me to the door. The children were curious but unresponsive.

Doctor Halikowski joined me, walking beside me in silence. He was a gentle, kind man, handsome despite the hardships with a sensitive face, now gaunt, with burning black eyes. His black hair was thick and tousled from lack of care. With it all, he did everything in his power to convey how he saw things until I interrupted.

"Doctor, I know something about Germans, their work marked my way across Europe. But, one thing I don't know; from a German's point of view, not a Nazi, an ordinary German if there was one, what would he say about Hitler Germany?"

"Ah yes, I see; well, we have one German, assists in laboratory, speaks English, once language teacher, Kurt Hentze. You come now, we shall see."

As we walked to the hospital, the bitter north wind, dry, dirty snow and paper scraps stung our faces with annoying force. The Doctor shouted louder than necessary relating the story of Kurt Hentze.

Kurt, like millions of other Germans, had witnessed the whole sordid Hitler mania. Early on he had watched and, finally, in the spring of 1939 he managed to enter Poland with his wife and remained, planning to become a citizen.

"Well, here is hospital…" The hospital was impressive; an old building, it reflected constant scrubbing and cleaning, giving off an odor of soap and disinfectant.

Doctor Halikowski walked quickly through the wide corridors, turning right, then left until we reached the rear entrance with a small office beside the outer door.

"Please to sit here, Kurt will come."

I took off my heavy coat, hung it on a wall hook and sat down behind a desk piled with folders and loose papers. The door opened; a tall, blonde, middle aged man stood motionless, one hand on the doorknob.

"Lieutenant Jim Hannon, United States Army."

"United States Army…" The German spoke the words slowly as he stepped in and closed the door.

"Kurt Hentze…"

"Sit down, thanks for coming."

Hentze took two long steps and sat down. A prominent forehead and incongruously small nose gave him, somehow, an ageless look.

"You really are American? From the lager?"

I nodded.

"What is it you wish with me?"

"If you don't mind, I've seen many remarkable things, some shocking and frightening. I wonder, what kind of people were they? How could it happen? If you can help me…" I spread my hands and waited.

Kurt stared at me as he answered, "Five marks."

I raised my eyebrows and waited. Kurt continued to stare until I repeated, "Five marks?"

The German relaxed noticeably and leaned back. "Five marks, the police pay five marks when you deliver an anti-Nazi word of a friend, relative or stranger you overheard on the street or anywhere. Five marks each time, so, if you have not heard it you make it up. Guilty or not, the person you have betrayed is in very bad trouble – and you have five marks."

"And that five marks enabled Hitler to become God?"

Kurt loosened his collar. "The significance of the five marks must not be overlooked. Even though they betrayed to win favor for themselves, of course, the five marks was nevertheless important. Faith and morals were systematically destroyed and replaced with lying, cheating, corruption, betraying and desire for more material things than ever dreamed of. Millions and millions of acres of good land in Poland and Russia and slaves, serfs, bound to the soil, all at no cost – people had no legal status. The Germans were beneficiaries of natural resources of a continent." He stopped and looked out the window.

"Please go on."

"The mental state of Germans – it is necessary for men to live together for mental health, to advance and prosper. To live with others is necessary to accomplish these things. A man alone, on an island, develops in a strange fashion; a child brought up without the company of other children becomes anti-social.

"This is what happened to Germany. A whole nation since 1914; there was no real contact with the western world; first, because of lack of money, then the Nazi government. Real contact with the west stopped in 1914; what does that mean? A generation not speaking to other western people, not studying western law, western history, western culture and all things other countries were doing.

"The western powers did not see the danger of this isolation. So, in twenty years a strange mentality developed causing a lack of faith in the world outside.

"I do not mean by a faith or belief in God – faith in man, in right and justice. They listen to the foreign radio at risk of life, but many do and are told they are 'Lies, all lies, propaganda'. So, there is no truth, no honesty, only degrees of cheating and betraying. This hopelessness makes them unreachable. You tell them things you have heard from B.B.C., you talk, you explain, they gaze at you, smile and say, 'My God, what a nice fairytale you are telling there'.

"The government rewards gross, black deeds, rewards bad qualities, rewards cruelty, pays five marks when you point at anti-Nazis. The most ghastly qualities of human nature have grown like weeds, killing off the goodness and by these bad things you can save your life.

"The capacity to hate and be cruel has developed in the German character during twenty-five years of material misery straight down to hell.

"I tell you about a German Officer in Poland, quite a gentleman, a Judge before, told me, quite simply, his task in a small district in Poland is to drive out of his district each week 150 farm families to make room for the Germans and he must now increase the numbers.

But, I asked, where are the 150 families to go? 'Oh well, that is not my job – to the forests, I guess'. I persist and ask what can they do in the cold winter? He laughed, a little bored with my childish questions, 'Well, I suppose they die, what else can they do?' A gentle man."

"Pardon me, Kurt, your answer to my question – five marks – how could it happen? Tell me, you implied more, much more than five marks made the great tragedy."

The answer came at once. "Five marks reveals everything about the regime and the people and why it was hopeless from the beginning. Think of it, your mind is stretched until it pains you; a nation of intelligent people could not resist planned corruption and the price, five marks, condemned them to total destruction.

"If ten people heard you criticize the government, one or more of them would betray you and be paid five marks. If you brought ten people into your home and you did not have a swastika or Hitler's picture in a prominent place or if it were small in size, one of them would betray you and receive five marks. If a boy heard his father late at night listening to the radio too often he would betray his father for five marks; if you told a Hitler joke, the man who laughed the loudest might be the one – for five marks.

"What about the German mentality and the German psyche? Is it different than the Englishman, the Frenchman or the American? Of course, because it has turned inward, conditioned to resist all sources of its nourishment unless it has approval of the Nazi Government.

"So, there becomes only one truth, Goebbels's truth, Himmler's truth, Goering's truth and, above all, Hitler's truth with nothing given to weigh against. Under that condition do you wonder what they believed coming from their leaders, what they rejected coming from their adversaries? What chance is there for truth and enlightenment in a national leader and a party who raises men's base qualities to earn special privileges and create millions of citizen informers?

"And then comes the moment of truth, the point of no return. Now it is too late to negotiate a peace; to stop fighting would ensure, perhaps forever, the end of the German nation. So, fight on, hopeless, yes, but so is surrender." He stopped and placed his hand over his eyes.

"I must go now back to work. It has given me pleasure to meet and tell what I know of my country's trouble. You are going home, think of my words and do what you can to make people understand. No one can progress in isolation. Think of it, five marks, and all the evil it can buy."

He stood a moment, head bowed, turning the doorknob one way and the other, then raised his head, staring unblinking. "I tell you something, Hitler understands what people are, he understands everyone has a price, not only Germans, everyone. When you speak of people, nations, political parties, nationality makes no difference. Give people what they want, tell them what they must do to keep what they have and, this saddens me, I believe they will do those things they are directed to do. Enough of them will carry out the order, 'befel ist befel', orders are orders, that is all that is required."

"I'll be leaving here. Germany will need men like you if you return. I wish you good luck."

I watched the tall man march down the long corridor; there was no other word to describe his stride. He marched, head high, until he reached a cross corridor where he turned abruptly to the left, slowed his pace, held up his right hand in a farewell gesture and was gone.

When he was out of sight a montage of images flooded my mind, then sorted out. The picture was coming into focus; a mixture of sympathy, anger, revulsion, compassion, forgiveness and condemnation – so many forces pulling me in so many directions I couldn't get a handle on it while I was a part of it.

Kurt Hentze had given me an answer, but with it a growing concern. To know the answer was to know the permanent nature of man's curse and the incurable depths of his weakness.

I stood up slowly, opened the door and murmured to myself, "Time to hit the road. 'Five marks,' is it possible?"

CHAPTER XXIII

Following a back road into the sparsely settled farm country, I looked back to the dark smudge on the horizon. Recent events prompted a surprising chain of thought. The person I had known and lived with for almost two years, the last months closer than any I had ever experienced, did not make our relationship anything more than what it was, a temporary thing tolerated in an environment and climate that offered no options.

The burden bearing down on me was an accumulation of overpowering loneliness and a mounting conviction that all life left to me might spill out at any hour in this desolate, ravaged country as it had for those...

My thinking process stopped when it came to me that those were bodies, all in a row, fifty feet off the road on a rise of ground surrounded by snow burdened pine trees.

As I walked toward them Teel said, "I'll wait while you investigate."

I stood at the end of the line looking at each of the German soldiers wearing great coats and helmets, their bare feet blue, frozen – the marble patina held my interest. Face up, side by side, there were twelve including a Feldwebel. Frozen expressions, strangely similar in death, showed no trace of fear, anger or pain. Numerous bullet holes crossed their upper torsos with a trickle of blood turned to ice here and there from a partially opened mouth.

Anonymous in death. I thought of those who mourned them, sustained by hope and savaged by fear, beginning a long wait that would have no end. My pent up emotions released in a burst of anger.

"There's no end, the whole world's a madhouse, five marks was the grease that kept the wheels turning."

Standing still, fists clenched, arms hanging straight down and face upturned, I swore aloud, "God help us..." and turned away.

By late afternoon our search for shelter became more urgent as the bleak valley began to meld with the coming night. The farm buildings were almost obscured; their outlines stood against a snow covered rise with a dim light source on one side.

An ancient crone peered out of the open door screeching and waving her hand.

"American soldiers, lager." Teel's shouted answer settled the issue. She went silent and motioned us inside, her yellow fangs and small darting eyes were as ugly as her temper.

An old man sat by the stove absorbed in two small dogs fornicating under the table.

It was a long evening. While the potato peel soup and black bread was filling, the lack of communication and whispered monosyllables between our hosts as they spooned their soup with coarse slurping noises added to the heavy, fetid atmosphere. I looked at Teel, pushed my dish away and laid my head on the table.

Later, we collapsed on a wide platform between the stove and a sidewall. I wondered at the warmth of the blankets not knowing the chimney ran horizontally under the width of the bed providing the source of heat.

At first light we got up and put on our greatcoats while the woman whispered and sent us sullen looks.

"Thank you pani, panyenka."

Teel stood at the door a moment looking to the east where the road turned and climbed into the foothills. A steady rumbling thunder held him there.

"We'd better keep it on the right..."

The wind from the east was on the rise pushing curtains of snow across the barren fields. I drifted back to that distant day when I joined the millions who had lost private citizen status. However it might have been for others, it was the source of endless self-doubt and mind wrenching.

I suffered with the knowledge that I might have evaded capture; I stayed too long with the Sergeant, moving upstream when I should have moved down, searching for concealment. Over and over I replayed the past until my anguish threatened to overwhelm common sense. I was left with glaring truth – my decision could not be reversed. And so it went, dimming, fading, until a bad moment would call it all back. I had woven the fabric of my life.

A long ago remark, tossed off by an old hand in the jungle brought a smile as I spoke it aloud, "The question isn't how did I get into this mess, it's how in the name of God do I get out?"

The past months had catapulted me into a climate where I was beset continuously with the dark side of man's nature; I had traded a traffic court summons for something that would tax the cerebral power of the Supreme Court.

The long swing of the road to the southeast brought the sound of heavy fire closer. Hunger and utter weariness had pushed us to the limit. We stopped, turned our backs to the wind and saw a truck. The unmistakable silhouette of a Studebaker with canvas top flapping was as familiar in Poland as it had been in Italy or North Africa.

It passed us and then slowed; we were over the tailgate before the wheels had stopped sliding. Two civilians sprawled on bulging flour sacks looked us over. Medium height and stocky, they wore black leather, fur collared coats, black fur hats and felt boots. Behind them the van was loaded with sacks of flour.

"Anglisher?" asked the older man.

I explained we were Americans, had been German prisoners and were concerned with the heavy gunfire.

The older man, with a gesture, said there was nothing to fear. He said all of the fighting was to the south and west of Dukla. The pass was free of troops, but there might be bandits or possibly some renegade German soldiers in the mountains, we could ride as far as Dukla with him and spend the night in his quarters. I asked his name.

Anduluski, he said, and then, with hand outstretched, introduced Stefan. Pulling a sack from between his feet, he dumped the contents on the waist high flour sacks, a bottle, a piece of cheese and a loaf of bread.

They kept pace as the bottle passed back and forth until Teel, holding a chunk of bread in one hand and a piece of cheese in the other, stopped chewing.

"You speak English like an American, how come?"

"Well, I am an American – still." He paused and studied his hands. "One of those people in the wrong place at the wrong time. I lived in Chicago, came to Poland to visit a grandmother I had never seen. She had not much time, June 1939, stayed too long, got trapped, so I make the best of it."

I smiled, "Chicago?"

Anduluski smiled back. "No, no gangster, I was a Chicago cop, a flat foot with ambition, years of night classes in criminal law. That made sense to me since I was working in the country's major crime laboratory." He spread his hands and laughed, "So, here I am, staying alive."

Between bites I asked how it was that a civilian could have a truck and gasoline. Anduluski laughed and made some remark about Poland, Russia or America, it made no difference; an enterprising man had to look out for himself and turn circumstances to his advantage.

During early evening we entered Dukla. The city was in ruins and crowded with Russian troops. As we approached the center of town, traffic increased until we were barely moving. The truck turned to the right before reaching piled up military traffic.

We passed shattered commercial buildings, several blocks of piled rubble and stopped beside a two-story building. We followed Anduluski, noting the deserted street, smashed windows and doors and the usual absence of lights or signs of life.

Anduluski knocked, waited a moment, spoke with someone on the other side and the door opened. We followed him and Stefan inside and up to the second floor.

The furnishings were impressive; upholstered chairs, fine rugs and large oil lamps with elaborate shades that gave a warm ambience to the room. Two young women took turns flinging themselves at Anduluski and exclaiming with much eye rolling as though he had been given up for lost doing his precarious business activities.

Unable to free himself, he literally dragged the girls with him as he escorted us to a bedroom and said we could rest until food and spirits were served. Taking turns, we washed up in a large porcelain basin then collapsed on the large bed, pulling up the blankets and closing our eyes.

"Yankee, come..."

Unable to waken Teel, I followed the girl as she led me down the dark corridor. She laughed as she interspersed her remarks with Yankee, Fred Astair, Clark Gable and others, all movie stars.

Dinner was sumptuous, served with an abundance of wine and spirits. I concluded my benefactor was living on the edge, walking a perilous line.

The two men had evidently not seen their girl friends for some time. Andulaski raised his glass and I raised mine – no words followed.

After they said goodnight, I drank coffee and enjoyed the luxury of my surroundings while contemplating good things to come.

Ginger came into focus, a vision that had sustained me throughout the times of trial and uncertainty, pushing away doubts and fears. I thought if she had not been there I would have invented her just as she was.

Memory sustained me and anticipation gave me boundless pleasure. There would be endless lovemaking and time to indulge ourselves in that unbelievable place, the Golden State. Sitting alone with the continuous rumbling rising and falling, I cherished the memory of a place and a lady far away, out of reach, tantalizing. I put down my cup, stood up, walked to the couch and laid down. "May the day come."

CHAPTER XXIV

Anduluski and Stefan were in high spirits during breakfast. Now and then they would speak in Polish, employing eloquent facial expressions, then laugh slyly and shake their heads.

Breakfast was a rare treat. Coffee Royals were dulling my appetite and apprehension even though the rolling artillery had become a continuous thunder rattling cups and glasses. We were not conscious of any urgency to get on with the journey.

When our host lit an after breakfast cigar I sensed the interlude was approaching an end. I asked the perplexing question that troubled me constantly, it marked every discussion with those who sheltered us regardless of status; the question was probably unanswerable.

"Can you explain the Volksdeutsche?"

At first, Volksdeutsche had made no lasting impression on me. A German was a German needing no further identification, but, as the road unwound, the word had taken on ominous meanings. Wehrmacht, Nazi, S.S. told me something of the characteristics of that highly compartmentalized world which must have been the strangest society ever created.

I had first heard the word when we sat in the little bakery with Cyna Jesionowski who told us there had been treacherous Poles, who had worked for the Germans. Along the way, others had set their faces in hard lines when Volksdeutsche came into the conversation.

Anduluski had been candid about many things, but when I asked him to explain the word he sat quietly for a long time, thoughtfully gazing out of the unwashed and cracked window. Finally, he inhaled deeply, blowing smoke rings that slowly ascended toward the ceiling. He seemed to be weighing, or perhaps evaluating, my question.

"Volksdeutche..." he paused for a moment, his eyes fixed on something behind me. "Only the Germans could have created such people, a class forever to be condemned. For those in an occupied country it was the ultimate offense, put in place by those who

151

practiced deceit and fraud, using flagrant lies and distortions in their dealings with all people, including their own.

"Here in Poland, the Volksdeutche were a means to an end, a class of Polish citizens striving to become German, which was not meant to be. In some territories a form of German culture was introduced; German was the language in schools and all institutions and offices of government were imitations of the Nazi, modeled after the super race.

"Those who did not elect to become German, the intelligentsia and property owners were removed. Those who remained fell into two classes, those who had chosen to become Germans and those who were permitted to remain as non-citizen serfs condemned to deliberate and constant humiliation. When he encountered a German uniform or someone with a badge or those who acted German the Pole must remove his hat and, if the encounter happened on a sidewalk, he must step into the street. A Pole could not travel by any conveyance, not even a bicycle. He did not have any legal status or protection whatsoever; all of his property was owned by the German authorities to dispose of as they pleased.

"Many professional and business people were imprisoned. More than half a million Poles were moved out of one district in the first two months of occupation followed by the great migration. From Germany hundreds of thousands arrived to appropriate what only months before had been personal property of the rightful owners.

"To add to the pain, all classes from peasant to artisan received a notice to move out of their homes within two hours, taking with them only a few personal things such as food and clothing. But that was not all, the homes had to be put in good order, cleaned and all their things, including their property, left for the new owners from Germany.

"Their children were made to prepare floral arrangements to be left on the tables and thresholds as a sign of welcome.

"All of these things could be avoided by the act of becoming one of them, one of the most select societies in all of Europe. That was the alleged reward if you became Volksdeutche, and that was a lie.

"How can we forgive them? They could not keep their place unless they served as they were directed. That included spreading lies, extolling the benefits available to Germans and, incredibly, spying and informing on countrymen, friends and family – so, they did it, the Volksdeutche."

His cigar had gone out unnoticed. I waited a moment before asking another question.

"There's something unexplained, unanswered about Germans. Maybe there isn't any answer. What they've done here makes me wonder if anyone really knows them. Is there something about their history that causes them to assert themselves as though they were put on earth by the almighty to shape and lead a way of life for all people? With their ridiculous strutting, shouting and boasting maybe they have an inferiority complex or a long standing sense of insecurity. What is it about them that creates the belief that they can push other people out of their own country and, eventually, out of the world?"

Anduluski's answer was restrained, his manner a little sad. "There are no bad people in the beginning. Among all other things they learn and believe are the things taught them at home, in school and, in a larger sense, in their national propaganda. All those things make up their total outlook until, in maturity, it is generally irreversible.

"Hitler's Aryan super race, military jingoism and chauvinism became a religion and, like religious fanatics, Germans became, over the years, racial fanatics, unresponsive to any rational, common sense regard for political alternatives. This was coupled with creating and defining inferior races and nations and removing other peoples from the protection of the law. Their monstrous efforts to establish themselves as superior to all peoples, laws and religions was successful — for a time. How could it happen? Hitler knew, he understood people; his enemies never understood his secret or him.

"Freedom is a myth, a bedtime story, it stops at the end of a bayonet. Some are permitted to keep the people believing the power and force at the top will work for them, it will never happen. Go play the song, mouth the words and protect your selfish interest; you can follow your star while you're winning."

Anduluski relit his cigar, then took a long draw. Tilting his head back, he blew a cloud of smoke upward, looked sideways at me and smiled.

"Hitler might have had his thousand year Reich, but, like Capone, he overreached, his wagon came unglued, the wheels came off in Russia. If he had buttoned up with what he had before Barbarossa, he would have had it made and in time, like the gangster laundering his money, might even have been forgiven for his crimes and become Chairman of the Board of Europe Incorporated."

I smiled, studied my hands and looked up at my host. "Do you think the memory of this war will prevent another?"

It was Anduluski's turn to smile. "My favorite writer is Shakespeare; I remember some lines from The Rape of Lucrece…

'Men's faults do seldom to themselves appear…their transgressions partially they smother…this guilt would seem death worthy in thy brother…'

"Who will remember and care enough in the years to come – the unspeakable agonies, the torrents of tears, the gnawing loneliness, the paralyzing terror of people counted in the millions? All of them were victims of a cruel regime and nation giving their hysterical support to their Fuehrer, a lunatic directing a powerful nation on a course of genocide, the madness that was Nazi Germany.

"Who will have time to care or remember? The victims are dust or soon will be. You know the line – the bad ones are gone, my best friend's a German, he's as angry with Hitler as you are. All profess innocence; it happened, it's over, let's get back to business. Besides, they'll be damned good allies if we need them."

I stared at Anduluski, my surprise was undisguised until he smiled and leaned across the table.

"Those aren't my feelings, but that's my view of things to come and, finally, I don't think this will be the last world war, it will be the second last."

Later, I mulled it over, knowing my own view of the world around me was becoming more uncertain as the debris of war and erosion of human rights mounted to distressing heights, hovering between a building optimism and a vague but strong sense of depression.

Teel sat down, poured coffee and spoke to Anduluski. 'I like your style, sir, thanks for the best night's sleep in memory."

"You'll soon be home and you'll see this place for what it is, the flatland after a Mississippi flood. Fill up, we'll be leaving shortly."

In mid-morning Anduluski announced he would drive east of the city to make certain we would be on the right road. Without any further ceremony, we got into our greatcoats, exited the building and climbed aboard the truck.

As we rolled along through the town we noticed many places were being used as hospitals. Many Russians were on walkways covered with blankets; the dead were carried on litters to open areas between buildings where they were laid in rows in their underwear with great red splotches coloring the area of their wounds.

Rumbling from the front had settled into a steady, heavy drumbeat.

"Niemcy still fights. Suicide, that's what it is for the Nazis to continue. Why does Hitler keep on fighting?" Anduluski showed little emotion other than the hint of a sneer when he spoke of Germans.

"We don't want you to get into trouble on our account, we'll find our way from here."

It didn't seem possible we could continue without someone becoming suspicious of the civilian chauffeured Army truck.

"It's all right, close to the front there is little to fear. Soldiers are too busy getting drunk or too worried about their own problems. Police have a hand in the black market business, there are many civilians employed to drive vehicles. When there is no fighting close by, there is much danger because then the troops suspect all civilians and question everyone."

He moved the sacks, lifted several out of place and returned with a straw-wrapped jug.

"You will not find this easy to come by when you leave Dukla. If you do not have misfortune, in three or four days you'll be all right. Drink only at night when you stop to rest. Keep your eyes open always while on the road."

"One for the road." Teel patted the jug.

Anduluski nodded his head in approval, then opened his coat and took out a large flat purse and selected several one thousand Zloty notes, placing them in my hand.

"Money is helpful, spend it before you cross the border. It may be worthless when you leave Poland."

I hesitated, "You've done many good things for us, we won't have a chance to repay you."

He looked out of the truck for a moment. "You can repay me, there's always someone who can't help himself. In America too, there are those who can't overcome misfortune. And now, we'll turn back!"

Anduluski shouted to the driver who turned the truck back towards Dukla, then waited with the motor idling.

"America has been good to the world." He spoke quietly.

I placed my hand on Anduluski's shoulder. "Good luck, stay alive, times will change."

Opening the jug, I held it out at arm's length. Anduluski took it and held it in both hands, looked at me and smiled as he raised it, "One for the road."

We drank quickly, shook hands all around, then walked away toward the white hills. Several hundred feet further on we stopped, turned and looked back. They were standing by the tailgate. Anduluski raised his gripped hands, we waved in response, starting up the hill as blobs of wet snow dropped off the branches and landed with a splash.

It was the time of day when the bleak and lifeless sameness of our view began to meld with the coming night; a hard time packed full of concern and depression, the emotional depths.

I had been on the road too long and seen too much misery, too much squalor and too much death. It came to me that's what war is all about; death is an industry devoted and designed to spread pain, hopeless deprivation, hunger, cold, sickness, all by-products of war. What would come after? Would there be an after or would it end with my feet sticking out of the snow beside a footbridge across a ditch like the German I'd seen back along the trail – was it Dukla? Sanok? Jarswow? Would someone search my pockets, find my address and send a note – 'We buried him with others where they fell, sorry for your trouble.' Maybe it would be better to never know.

CHAPTER XXV

Continuous thunder from the south diminished as we rounded the first cut. The grade increased and the forest thickened cutting visibility, adding to our fear of meeting desperate Germans traveling west.

When the cut narrowed the snow deepened and we were forced to a slower pace. Speaking in single words, we tried to hold to the center while fighting the grade. We hoped to reach shelter before dark, knowing night would come early in the heavily wooded ravine.

As the first long shadows closed above, several rifle shots split the silence. We stood still, riveted in place, not able to determine the direction of the echoing, sharp burst. The way forward had nothing to recommend it, but, finally, we chose to go on and then stopped when a familiar sound filled the canyon.

The truck slowed as it came into sight and stopped. A Russian leaned out the window, looked us over, shouted something in Russian and then added, "Macaroni?"

I laughed and shouted in turn, "Amerikanski, nyet Macaroni."

He grinned and waved us aboard. Apprehension brought on by the coming night and the oppressive loneliness evaporated as we climbed aboard the Studebaker, feeling something close to a proprietary interest.

We settled back against the sideboards, then saw the white-cloaked soldier, immobile, his back to the cab, rifle across his knees.

He looked steadily at me. I pulled the jog of Vodka from the burlap sack and he accepted the bottle with a nod. He took a long drink, several long breaths, another drink and handed it back.

I swallowed a mouthful of the spirits marveling at the soldier's ability to put it down without any visible reaction.

The combination of the extraordinary breakfast and long session with Coffee Royals capped by hours on the uphill road and, finally, the potent spirits from the jug caused me to slowly cross over into my refuge, reliving an interval long gone.

* * *

In a state under the surface of consciousness I saw her, vivid, warm, crowding out of my mind the events that had made up the days and nights long past. The full impact of her memory brought back all the sweet delights and warm pleasures of our time together.

She stepped into the train station as I approached and turned toward me; I stared, unmindful of my manner as she smiled and waited. At that moment, seeing her and remembering, the word exquisite struck me; it was made for her.

I remembered the soaring feeling of the first hours without the usual awkward silence. She had, with her natural grace, revealed her delight in seeing me again. We planned little beyond the next hour, day or week and the vagary of the future never interfered with the wondrous days and nights of gratification and fulfillment.

She lay facing me, asleep. The pale moonlight entering through wide-open windows, imparted an appearance so fragile that had it not been for the warmth of her body and the gentle motion of her bosom I might have thought her lifeless.

I loved to watch her face at such times, her eloquent expressions and her frenzied, exquisite excitement. The bed, the room, every visible thing was in motion, faster, whirling, ascending. The barrier would hold fast for a time and then give way all at once to our combined assault. Then the tranquil descent, together, always together, pressed close. I waited as she finally fell asleep listening to the rhythm of her soft breathing.

When time was running out, we took the vows and found a wonderful sense of oneness and a bonding knowing whatever was to come would be shared. We talked of love and many things that came of it, but seldom of the past or the time that would come after. Those short weeks were a gift of unspoiled rapture.

The last dawning I dressed quickly, stood over her for a moment, then left her, walking hurriedly down the broad avenue, uncertain in the cold silence of early morning.

Late afternoon we met in the military air terminal, worked through the crowd and stood on the broad steps while people hurried past. All that could be said was done with. Her tears flowed as we embraced; a long kiss and I hurried away. When I reached the plane, I turned, raised my hand and she waved; it was my last sight of her as the crowd closed in.

* * *

I reached for the bottle. "Everyone loses!" My shout got the Russian's undivided attention.

After a pull on the bottle, I held it out to the soldier who was looking at me in a suspicious way. Despite his attitude, he reached for the bottle and drank without taking his eyes off of me. Slowing and turning off the highway, the truck moved over a series of potholes and steep rises until it stopped with a lurch.

The soldier went over the tailgate without a word. We followed the Captain and driver down the slope to a group of buildings almost invisible among the pines in the gloomy shadows. The white-cloaked soldier moved out to a flank position, rifle at the ready.

While we were approaching the dwelling, a door opened. Two men walked toward us smiling and exclaiming over the Captain. It occurred to me it wouldn't have mattered had the Captain been German, Japanese or a man from Mars – the greeting would have been the same. War does strange things to people. I had discovered civilians had one cardinal rule in common; don't offend men with guns no matter the color of their uniforms.

The Captain's words, in Polish, were delivered with force and received with visible concern.

The kitchen, dining room and sleeping room entity was unusually large with a typical low ceiling that held the smoke and odors, creating a stale atmosphere. Three women, chattering and smiling, cleared the long plank table and benches.

Greetings finally concluded, the Captain spoke to his men who hurried outside and returned with sacks and a straw covered demijohn. They placed dark loaves of bread, a slab of pork fat, a bag of sugar, a carton of tea and the demi-john on the table.

With a sweeping gesture, Russian Captain Borchoff invited all present to sit down. We did, with ravenous attacks on the fare. Afterwards, the Vodka received the same treatment.

The talk might as well have been carried on in Chinese for all we cared. Enough Vodka had been consumed by all present to remove any inhibitions, so they talked about things of interest to themselves.

"I am Anna," she said as she eased onto the bench. She waved her hand over the table, "They talk of war, of course, that's all we know for five, six long years. You are American? German prisoners, no?"

"We were prisoners. Your English is very good."

"Yes, I taught English to Polish Junior Officers at the Polygon in Rembertov, that is across the river from Warsaw after Praga."

I smiled, "Of course, I was there. It is something else now, a refugee camp."

She was not listening. All the others, except Captain Borchoff had stopped talking, they were leaning on the table looking intently at Borchoff.

Anna turned her head. "Leftenant, let me translate, 'Never can we equal the score, never, through all the ages has the world seen such barbarians'."

Borchoff paused to refill his mug.

Anna faced me, "The Captain is eloquent, this may be very interesting—he is deliberate."

"We followed close on to the retreating Von Runstedt's Army Group South, between the Bug and the Dnieper southeast of Rostov, coming on to something…" He paused and lit up another Lucky Strike; his eyes burned like hot coals.

"In the vast emptiness of the Crimea bordering the Ukraine, the undulating steppe stretched to a junction with the unsoiled blue of the heavens. There, the Nazi's put down something borrowed from Dante's Inferno, a profaned place, obscene, surrounded with electric charged wire, towering guard platforms manned by Wehrmacht who relieved their boredom by firing, without provocation, indiscriminately into the massed hordes of Russian prisoners baking under the burning sun."

Borchoff looked around the table, coming to rest on me, then continued with Anna translating.

"Prisoners, helpless, packed together, living out their death sentence – starvation. Two hundred thousand men in the heart of their homeland, ravaged by hunger, with untended wounds and in all stages of dying sending up to the heavens their heartbreaking cries. It was a sound carried by the wind across the steppe, eerie, terrible, and haunting, diminishing as the suffocating heat thinned the ranks, a monstrous harvest exacted by a force capable of surpassing each confounding atrocity with something more horrific.

"No shelter, no medicine, no food, no mercy, all designed to achieve a purpose, isolate, deny, then, in due time, the problem solves itself. They will cry, beg, call out, scream for their mother and implore; no matter, they will die.

"The living, outside the wire, were afraid. The sound was like nothing ever heard; if you have not known such a sound, you cannot imagine it.

"Two hundred thousand dying men, a hair raising chorus, begging the powers to relieve their agony and no one to respond; few would live to tell.

"All day and all night the wailing, without pause, until the cattle, the dogs and even the birds are restless, feeling the terror.

"Those who hurled themselves into the wire were left cooking until they blackened and dried up.

"Day and night, the haunting, uneasy stirring rose and fell as a ghastly miasma soiled the atmosphere across miles of haunted steppe."

Captain Borchoff stood up casually, nodded to us and raised his hand to the others. A long silence followed after he was gone.

Anna noticed my head drop, and then come up sharply. I smiled and explained, "Long hours out of doors, Vodka, food, warmth inside. I'm sorry."

"Come, no need to explain."

She directed me to a platform between the stove and hearth, straightened the blankets and sat down. Those at the table extinguished the lamps and moved into rooms at the far end. Pine logs in the hearth had burned down to a bed of embers.

I stood, unsure, as Anna took my hand.

"Rest, dream of home and all the pleasures waiting. This old land and the people are tired, worn out, but we still hope and dream."

The soft light from the coals pushed back the hard years, working a remarkable change. She was an extremely handsome woman, striking patrician features, piled ash blond hair and the hint of a smile.

She sat down facing me and motioned toward the door, "They are asleep, your friend has a bed and you will sleep here beside the fire."

"Is this your home, Anna?"

"It's our home, all of us. The owners are with the others in the snow. I want to tell you when you leave, forget us, forget Poland. We are glad to meet Americans; I have watched and listened to you speak. Lieutenant, you have feeling, you suffer in your way without complaint." She reached out and touched my hand.

"You can't help us, we are beyond helping. The Germans did their work well. They drove caring and trusting out of people, even among ourselves."

She smiled, stood up and left the room.

In the morning I awakened and sat up motionless until I had my bearings, then went outside to the forest and washed in a small creek. Hunger pangs hurried my return.

Smoke from the big stone chimney dropped almost to ground level and floated across the open field to the highway.

Anna and the other women had placed food on the table as noises from the adjoining rooms hurried their work. Teel sat by the fire sipping coffee.

She poured from a large pot hanging in the hearth and sat beside me, her warm mood still in place.

"Captain Borchoff remembers too much."

"How is that possible, Anna? I would hope all German victims would remember. I'm sure you have memories that will stay forever."

She sat the coffee mug on the table. "Would you care to see? Come."

Leading me to a narrow footbridge across a deep gully at the edge of the forest, she walked halfway across, stopped and pointed first to one side and then the other of the streambed.

"The work of the barbarians."

Bodies were visible on both sides of the stream in places where the snow had melted.

"Niemcy was retreating, there were many foot soldiers, tanks and trucks. They gathered up Polish people, men and women. They called them hostages. I was one of them, we knew we were expendable.

"Sounds of gunfire behind us were closing. They stopped the column there on the road. We were herded to this place, some across the bridge, down the bank on both sides, then came the firing from the bridge and there on the banks; hand bombs were thrown down into the packed prisoners. The nightmare continued until shouted commands from the road called them back."

Anna loosened her scarf and pulled down her sweater, exposing a livid, red scar cutting across her neck.

"I remained still among the others. Later, the sounds from the road were gone. Some of us survived, men in the house and the women, not many, others are still there."

Again she pointed to the contorted bodies. "Come, there is something else."

Crossing the bridge, we followed a rutted road into the tall pines. Anna stopped as the ground fog thinned in the clearing ahead where the sun poured out a welcome warmth clearing the ground of all but a few drifts of packed snow.

Foundations and chimneys with blackened timbers hanging from perches around the perimeters were the remains of the small village.

"Woodcutters and shepherds, simple mountain people, no threat to anyone. Still, the German culture was so strongly implanted the reaction was habitual. Those who shot us also destroyed this place. Come..."

She took my arm and walked to the center of the clearing through the charred debris and sour smell of burned out ruins.

A waist high fieldstone well poked up out of black-crusted snow. As we closed the distance, I saw the well piled to the top with bundled shapes; we were standing close enough to touch them.

Bullet riddled bodies, twisted and frozen in place were pressed tightly together, their clothing pulled one way and another. Limbs at grotesque angles of men and women, their blood turned to ice on their faces.

Reaching straight up between a knee length boot and the top of a head, my eyes fastened on a tiny, marble-like hand, fingers still clutching a crust of bread.

"Kinder too?" I asked, not wanting to hear the answer.

"Of course, we did not know then, the firing came while we were shouted down the bank. I saw the black smoke above the trees and then our turn came."

The doll-like fingers and tiny arm, blue with frost, bore deep into my mind, submerging a burgeoning optimism born in the hour's just past.

Something, perhaps fear, held me motionless. We walked to the house in silence. Close to the entrance, Anna turned to me.

"Leftenant, I have written my name and address here, send me word when you are safely home. During these times we make temporary friends and go our separate ways, without sadness at parting, and soon these chance meetings fade away almost unremembered."

She took my hand and looked up into my eyes. "That is the nature of the times, you do not fit the pattern. I will remember you, God speed your journey in safety."

I took her gently in my arms, kissed her and then held her at arm's length.

"I will write whenever this journey ends. You are special, Anna, I won't forget you."

The others were at the table. A tantalizing odor of ersatz coffee and fried bread lightened the mood as I sat down across from Captain Borchoff who nodded as he spoke to Anna.

"The Captain wants to know how is your life in America?"

I put down my cup. "Very good, I lived in the State of Washington with its snow covered mountains, evergreen land, forests, farms, orchards, Puget Sound and Pacific Ocean and then moved to California. I didn't realize how good it was until I came to the old world. Now I wish the whole world, all of it, was America and people from all over the world could live together in peace."

Captain Borchoff raised his cup and smiled, "Noz Drovia."

CHAPTER XXVI

The soldier sat as before, silent, both hands clenching his rifle. Absorbed in the black top road unwinding through turns and grades, free of snow, the kilometers spun off as shafts of sunlight filtered down through towering pines. I was at peace with myself; Teel was asleep.

"It's ending just like it began, with a rush. I've made it, the last round."

I smiled at the soldier staring at me, listening to the strange words coming from what must have been in his view a strange man.

When the sun was over the forest on the western side of the road, the truck slowed, pulled off the road and stopped. We followed the soldier over the tailgate.

A chain barricade stretched between two posts across the road; on the eastern side there were several small buildings. Russian soldiers were talking to Captain Borchoff.

On the slope, side-by-side, were two large display poster paintings of decorated Russian generals. I waited beside the tailgate until the Captain shouted and beckoned to me.

With obvious pride, a Sergeant of the guards pointed to the General on the left, "Kon-ee-ev." Then he gestured to the other, "Boodyanee."

I responded, "Dobra, Marshals Koniev and Budyenny."

"Da –da…" He pointed toward the chain barrier, "Slo-vak-ee."

Holding up both ungloved hands, fingers extended, he pushed his hands close to me, "Metzeelaborsk…"

I repeated the message, "Metzilaborce, ten kilometers."

Borchoff signaled the driver, the truck turned back with its motor idling. He handed us a loaf of bread and a large chunk of cheese. As a guard unlocked the chain and pulled it to one side, Borchoff waved his men aboard. Slapped us on our backs, climbed into the cab and shouted, "Ou-S-Ah, dobra."

We watched the truck until it dropped out of sight, turned and walked into Czechoslovakia.

"Ten kilometers maybe." Teel commented.

Our pace quickened as the silence packed in around us. My thoughts ran to the dark side, memories of things along the way came together as a towering cumulus cloud covered the setting sun.

The living were usually concerned with matters of the moment, food and shelter. After that they could get their second wind, recharge, fill up their tanks and put tomorrow in perspective. Whatever might have been was beyond recall.

Just then the sun burst through a rift in the overcast dissolving the gloomy half-light, lighting up a long white valley running between evergreen borders to a distant ridge.

Shading my eyes from the glare, my mood changed as thoughts of the good things to come were almost close enough to touch. The feeling grew.

Hours later, moving wearily up an interminable winding grade, we heard the deep roar of heavy bombers. Searching the sky, we found them. Large, four motored planes were crossing the valley. They were low enough to identify the white-bordered blue star and the USAF on the underside of the wings. Although we knew no one up there could see us, still we shouted, waved and laughed until tears filled our eyes. Pouring out my gratitude and thankfulness, I shouted, "You lovely bastards!"

Teel shouted. "There's our ride home."

The bombers were letting down for an airfield somewhere on the other side of the mountain pass.

In late evening, we saw a small barn in the center of an open field of snow surrounded by tall pines.

"There's our hotel buddy, let's get settled before dark."

Pushing through the deep snow, we reached the door and pulled it open; it was piled halfway to the rafters with hay. we closed the door. Searching in the half-light, we found horse blankets and crawled to the far wall where we dug into the hay, spread the blankets, laid down, covered ourselves with another blanket and piled on hay.

"Rest and think the good thoughts."

"Tell me a bedtime story, I won't interrupt."

"If you do, the floor's yours, as they say in Congress."

"None of...sorry, get on with it."

"April, worst of winter was over, a mild spring, snow was gone, most of it. I flew with a famous bush pilot, Shorty Russick, in a Gruman Goose..."

"In it or on it?"

"I'll ignore that – Cordova to Fairbanks, that's Alaska, met an Engineer on the boat, boarded in Seattle. Ship's name was S.S. Alaska, seems appropriate, don't you think?"

"Am I supposed to believe this?"

"Gospel truth, Pat, I moved around a lot, left a job on the Coulee Dam project in western Washington. They had me on the face of a cliff in a bosun's chair drilling holes with a Jack Hammer, when I moved up or down the man in the bosun's chair beside me filled the hole with sticks of dynamite – that's another story, let's go back to Alaska."

"You're pushing me, Jim"

"That's the only way to do it, the way it happened. Want me to go on?"

"Let's have Alaska."

"I was looking for a job, so was everybody else it seemed. Sitting in a deck chair watching the scenery, they call it the Inside Passage, believe me we squeezed by cliffs so close you could reach out and strike a match. Then we were running through heavy fog, pea soup a deckhand called it, the whistle was blowing and I asked the deckhand how they could navigate. He said they put a stopwatch on the whistle, time how long it took for the echo to bounce back, then they would know how close they were to land. Pretty scary, Pat. On the return trip we hit, but there I go, anyhow, an elderly, well dressed gentleman sat down in the next chair."

"Why do you call him a gentleman?"

"He looked like one."

"What does a gentleman look...never mind."

"They look different than truck drivers or carpenters, turned out he was a Civil Engineer on his way to Esther Creek to mine gold. Very interesting, he built drag lines, monsters, all electric with giant pontoons on each side and the hull in between they raise the hull, it moves, sets down, they call them walking drag lines."

"How do you know so much about them?"

"Mister Parsons, the gentleman, hired me. We built one, all steel; matter of fact the ship I was on carried the steel, unloaded in Anchorage then loaded on the Alaska Railroad. When it was put together the 'A' frame was seventy feet high from ground to pulley."

"I know there's something going to happen that I'm not going to believe, get to it."

"As a matter of fact, something quite remarkable, Hydraulic mining, I handled a nozzle shooting water under high pressure into the other side of Esther Creek washing away sedimentary deposits so the drag line could mine the gravel bed underneath, get the picture?"

"That figures – I'm just getting to the punch line and you're asleep, talked myself into it. Sleep well."

* * *

I sat up; the earlier sound of rising wind had diminished. Propped against stanchions, I broke off chunks of bread and cheese while looking through the door. The blue sky and tall, evergreen trees scattered across a dazzling, unbroken stretch of fresh snow brought a flood of memories.

The New World, Europe's name for that distant place holding promise for millions who would never, ever enjoy its everlasting innocence.

An end and a beginning to all things. I was sobered by the suddenness of its coming. It had begun that way, passing through each stage until the attack on Pearl Harbor, the lightning stroke that had changed my life.

Sandoval and a quick burst of machine gun fire at Salerno, Turner at Anzio walking carefully behind the shattered walls of the villa; the sniper had just that one moment when he passed the opening that had been a doorway – it was enough.

Then, for a long, wonderful, interminable time I thought of pleasures savored, dreams beckoning urging me home. Slowly, I settled back and closed my eyes.

Lying quietly, my thoughts were drawn to things of the past, vivid and alive. Harvest on the Kansas prairie, fights in those young days, their importance lessened by what followed. I remembered how determined I was to get even, give back in brutality what I had received and how soon that view faded and became unimportant.

I thought about the simple loyalties, the freedom of my thinking process, beginning all the way back to those first years in St. Paul certain now it was the same everywhere for everyone.

My country, my way is better than yours, I am strong because I am right and I am good and my God is the only God. Pride was as much a part of man's life as his religion or nature's seasons. Nothing, not one thing I had witnessed in my long journey could destroy my optimism, it had sustained me as the melancholy cry of all the profaned victims settled back into the ashes of the long war. The shocking thought that a man could send another to hell for *five marks* caused me to grope with reality.

I floated back into a drowsy indifference and slept until a flock of raucous crows chose the roof for a rendezvous.

Awaking refreshed, with an astonishing feeling of well being, I lay quietly for a moment contemplating my good fortune. I smiled and stretched luxuriously. The vista through the open shed door was bright and clear and Teel was still asleep.

Slowly, I got up, leisurely brushed the straw from my coat and hair and walked to the door, surveying the scene as I moved cautiously into bright sunshine.

A light snowfall had filled in our trail from the road to the barn. I took a step out of the shadows and stopped. For a moment I looked across the unmarked white surface, around the verdant border, then up to grading shades of blue crowning my first glimpse of freedom since the black day at Anzio. It was not yet in hand, but I felt it.

I tossed my pack up in the air, ran out of the shadows and sprawled full length in the snow. Rolling over, I stood upright, arms outstretched, head thrown back.

Shouting incoherently, I ran in circles until finally collapsing on my back. Standing up, I yelled at Teel.

"Pat, you're forgiven for everything, wake up, wake up!"

The sound of an aircraft came all at once. One moment an unbroken silence, the next the pulsing roar of the motor. Searching the sky, I saw the small bomber flying from the lower end of the valley. When it passed, I looked up smiling, shouting a greeting and waving. I could see the two pilots and, for the first time, noticed the black swastika on the fuselage. They waved back a scant hundred feet over my head and then I saw the bubble under the tail and heard the gun.

With one hand still held aloft, I watched the little puffs of snow race toward me across the meadow and pass me by two paces removed.

"Wake up, it ain't over."

I walked back into the barn. "I have a feeling we're going to make it."

"That son-of-a-bitch tried to end it." Teel shouted.

"Listen, listen hard…"

There was a long unbroken silence – I raised my hand, "I hear aircraft."

The sound of aircraft engines was loud and clear. When they topped the western ridge I shouted, "They're ours, air cooled engines, another squadron same as the others, B-17's."

Three abreast, too high to read the letters, the white star was visible under the wings and on the side of the fuselage. Teel sprawled on his back in the soft snow laughing and shouting.

"Jesus, what a sight for these tired eyes. Believe me, buddy, we'll never top this, lines of heavies like they're on parade. Where they're pointed we're going, watch 'em, they're coming down."

"You've got that right, I make it northeast."

I studied the map LaBorce had given me. "Here it is, we're here somewhere, Hungary or Rumania. It's Rumania, that's it, a target for the first time since I had the bad luck to run into you."

Teel punched my shoulder, "I'm rescued, won't have to listen to anymore of your hippity hoppity, crazy made up stories."

We embraced then plowed through the snow to the clear, blacktop road. The last echelon of bombers sank below the eastern hills.

Mid-afternoon, when the chill predicted a hard night, the sound of a motor brought us to a stop. We stood on the shoulder watching the smoking vehicle approach then moved to the center of the road and raised our hands. It slowed to a stop, the door opened and the driver leaned out shouting in a new language.

I walked close, smiled and answered, "Americanski, Kreigsgefannen, lager, Officier."

"Ah, good, speak English, my cousin Neebraska, yes, good, good, O.K." He laughed, leaned over and opened the other door.

The interior was a shambles, no seats, just boxes, sacks, pieces of wood, pipe and buckets.

"Sit on box, sacks, we have good day, Metzilaborce one hour, maybe two." He laughed as he pulled away, not fast enough to run away from the exhaust fumes filling the interior.

"Where you go?"

Teel leaned close to the driver and shouted, "Your exhaust pipe is broke."

"Name Gregor, you hear, no pipe."

"Pat Teel, Jim Hannon."

Gregor reached back, moved boxes until he uncovered a bottle, pulled it loose with his elbows on the steering wheel and pulled the cork out with his teeth.

"Gregor make brandy."

He tipped the bottle, drank, and then handed it to me.

"Make good brandy, yes?"

Teel reached for the bottle. "Only thing I judge by is results, yes?"

Choking on the drink, he laid back on the sacks while I struggled with the window handle; it turned but the window didn't move.

"Did Tedeschi fight here?"

"Fighting tanks, soldiers, family far away. They come to house, understand smokehouse?"

"Where you smoke the hams, right?"

"So, they take hams, salt pork, all, break machines, shoot animals behind barn, milk cow behind house."

"For the meat?"

Gregor shook his head, pounded the steering wheel with both hands. "No meat, just kill."

He pointed to a livid scar on his forehead. "Captain with pistol strikes, I am down by cow, they laugh, make fire, wheat gone in fire, finished."

The noise and fumes ended the conversation. We dozed until Gregor touched my shoulder.

"Here, stop."

"Where are we?"

"Here I sleep, then Metzilaborce – enjoy Gregor brandy." He spread his hands and smiled.

I opened the door and we got out. Teel reached for Gregor's hand. "You're a good man."

We crossed the Hungarian border two days later; the border station was unoccupied. A weathered map painted on the side of the building showed towns and cities.

I placed my finger on Miskoch. "Our next stop, buddy, and traffic is scarce."

Weather was our challenge; cold, bone chilling cold brought us down. We were without options, our morale struggled with our depression.

Afternoon traffic was light, going the wrong way; occasional farms and outbuildings were far from the road. We hugged a tree line or any low place hidden from sight. Like everything else on our journey, it seemed, the resident farmers were private people, hunkered down in their cozy cottages.

Straight ahead a black cloud hugging the ground was growing fast and a strong, cold wind hit us straight on; in minutes a blizzard drove us off the road. We spotted a barn on a side road and ran for it before it vanished in the storm.

The door was partially open, hanging askew; swirling dust and straw particles filled the interior and the side windows were without glass. We ruled it out.

"Pat, this side road leads somewhere, there must be a house close by."

"Makes sense, if it's not close to the road we'll never see it."

"Let's go."

Our luck was in; minutes later, a typical house with a thatched roof was close enough to hit with a rock. Following the wall past a window we located a door. I knocked, waited, knocked again and shouted.

"Ou S Ah – Americanski – soldier – from Lager."

"Show me something."

We turned away from the door

A tall, slender boy, bare headed, carrying a rifle with bayonet stood two paces removed. I bared my wrist showing my bracelet and shouted. "My name and Army serial number – we are U.S. Officers, escaped from a German Lager, Schubin, Poland."

He smiled. "Come, follow me, I am Steven."

"O.K., Steven, I'm Jim and this is Pat."

He led us around to the back door into a well kept big room with a large iron stove against the back wall, a wood table scrubbed almost white and four chairs in the center of the room. The odor of baking bread was overpowering.

Near the far end of the stove a grey haired lady was seated in an upholstered chair holding a cane in her left hand; she stared at us as Steven spoke.

"We are Brezinskis, mother, sister Neda and I. Our Priest study at Notre Dame, U.S.A., he gave me English since I was a child. Your coats, hats and sacks – please now sit."

Steven helped his Mother out of her chair and into her room.

"A good family; seems the father's missing."

Steven returned and sat opposite them. "What will happen now?"

Pat nudged me with his knee.

"We go on until we find transport, eventually American troops."

"There – here there is only Russian, they will help you – no?"

"We have met Russians, they have helped us but still we have not found transport to start us on our way home."

"So it is, our father is gone, he was Major – Polish soldier. Now we have Neda, meet sister Neda – here American soldiers, were German prisoners – Jim here and Pat."

Neda was a striking young lady. She resembled her brother; tall and slender, blonde hair, her long-sleeved blue dress matched her blue eyes. We stood until she was seated; her smile was genuine.

"A   beautiful   young   lady,   we   are   honored   Neda."

"English no, not a word. Now I tell you how it was with the Germans – here we are what you see, Mother, Neda and Steven, my father, Steven Brezinski, was taken when Tannenberg fell, nothing we have heard, four years now. Mother Brezinski prays – I believe not – Father will not return. Look at me – understand?"

I nodded. Pat said, "Go on."

"We have enemy here harvest time, they were bad. From above I saw, heard loud voices, screams. I died, not can help. How to say – a child will come to our house summertime – understand?"

Pat tensed, his fists clenched; I touched his arm.

"Steven, we want your mailing address, you will have a letter when we get back to America, write it now please – understand?"

173

"Yes, post, letters, I have such things. Now you will eat, Neda will help."

Without effort it seemed, the table was set and we were served ham, mashed potatoes, red wine and, a first, white bread and butter.

"Neda wants you to know American movies, Fred Astaire, Cagney and Gable – no? Again, war finished, we see American movies – yes?"

"We miss our movies too, Steven, it won't be long until both wars will end. Germany and Japan are destroyed, peace will come this year."

Pat held out his package of cigarettes; Steven hesitated then pulled one out, turned it one way and another, took the light I offered, drew on the cigarette, and then exhaled.

"America, all things there good, good."

With the warmth, a full dinner and the end of daylight our endurance ebbed.

Steven smiled, "O.K., bed, come, sleep now."

As usual, sleep came at once. The next thing I knew sounds from the big room got me out of bed.

Sunshine flooded the room; we dressed hurriedly. Neda was putting dishes on the table. She was a rare reminder of someone waiting halfway around the world; her pregnancy was visible.

We followed Steven outside for morning duties.

"Neda shows her secret."

"No secret, Jim – no German baby – O.K. – Hungarian baby – O.K.?"

"O.K., makes sense."

Breakfast finished, Mother Brezinski handed Steven a paper. He waited, looked at his mother, then read.

"'Major Steven Brezinski died of pneumonia this day, two two November 1942, signed Major Johann Krause.' We do not believe, this come from Debrecen."

He put his finger on the post imprint. "Your father was not Polish?"

"Father, Mother, Neda, Steven all Polish. Why in Hungary? We are here much years – this farm came to Father – how to say – family – his family, that is how."

A look from his Mother caused Steven and Neda to take her away.

"Jim, let's give them our Czech money."

"Good thinking – good food, a good sleep, sunshine – what are we waiting for?"

"Ever think you wouldn't know what day it is, where you are, where you're going and when you'll get there?"

Our laughter was cut short when Steven returned. Rummaging in a corner chest, he pulled out a pillow cover, stuffed it with a loaf of bread then added another, a chunk of cheese and a large slab of white fat. Steven tied a knot, shook hands and said, "Mother Brezinski not good, I go find medicine."

"Thanks for your hospitality, tell your Mother the war will end this year and, incidentally, we want you to have this money. Tell Neda we wish her well – they're in good hands. Steven."

Walking towards the highway, we stopped and turned back; Steven and Neda were standing in the doorway, hands raised. We returned the salute, adjusted our bindles and turned onto the Miskoch Highway.

CHAPTER XXVII

Every vehicle was westbound including loaded Studebaker personnel carriers and Jeeps, also loaded.

"Dammit, Jim, I know we're going the wrong way, hell, we're running out of towns and people. It's not too late to turn around."

"Not me, big cities are coming up, Miskoch, Debrecen, Budapest – one of them has what we're looking for, U.S. troops, and then, my friend, we go west in style by air. We'll be home before we run out of Luckies."

Long days were becoming a habit; we were ignoring our long held cardinal rule – bed down before dark. It was night, pitch black when we entered the western fringe of Miskoch.

"Don't like it, Jim, we can see outlines of buildings but where are the lights? It's weird."

"You've got that right – and no traffic."

"Should have stayed with Steven, sometimes talking and asking questions helps. This is a graveyard."

"Cool it, Pat, we're doing fine, no artillery fire. I hear a motor – there he is, coming off a side road – he's turning this way."

We moved to the side of the road, the truck slowed and stopped. Someone shouted and we were surrounded by uniforms. A tall soldier approached, held out his hand and spoke; I answered not knowing what he said.

"U.S.A.,Americans–Kreigsgefannigen."

I pulled up my sleeve and raised my wrist.

"Major Bodony, Commandant Polees."

He spoke to his troops; they tied our arms and herded us to the side of the truck, turned us around to face the Major. In clear English, his voice was barely above a whisper and, to our amazement, he was with us.

"You must not stop here, my Chief is pro-German, a Nazi. I can take you to the border, Romania. There you will find American Air Force. So, good luck, across the border find shelter, load up now."

I put a pack of Luckies in his hand. Hopefully, we would find transport before we ran out of our magic Luckies.

Bodony leaned close, his whisper barely audible. "O.K., U.S.A., O.K."

We loaded up, crossed the border, dropped to the road and the last we saw of Major Bodony was the palm of his hand raised toward us as we shouted, "So long, Major."

"I don't believe it, Jim, so help me God."

"We're here, in Romania – we're going to make it, Pat."

"As Bodony would say, is goodbye – no?"

Turn your head – look up there, under the moon."

There was a silhouette on the top of a hill off the road a mile or two; twin towers with a large outline between.

"It's a castle, older than baseball."

"And then some, looks abandoned, want to try?"

"You mean…?"

"Here's the turn off."

"I don't know, Jim."

"Come on, maybe Count Dracula will meet us at the gate."

"To hell with you, Jim, that does it."

As we closed the distance the road became a series of switchbacks. At the top, one half of a massive gate was open. We entered and stopped, it was an enormous structure, no lights or signs of occupants; the yard was a mess with scattered debris, rocks and broken furniture.

"The king of the hill is about to meet Count Dracula."

"That's not funny, Pat."

A stone paved court was a series of potholes and debris leading to wide stairs and a large wood door with metal straps.

"I don't know, think about it."

"I have, Pat, I'm tired and cold, willing to share a fire and cigarette with Dracula. I need your muscle."

I tried the latch; we leaned and pushed until it opened partially then stuck fast.

"I have a question, Jim, why are we doing this?"

"Because there's a big fireplace in there and, hopefully, some logs. We'll have a roaring fire, toast some bread, a couple shots Gregor's brandy and wait for daylight. How does that grab you?"

"Better than the cemetery."

Leading the way, I stumbled. "Light a match, this is where our luck changes."

"Which way?"

The light gave us a quick glimpse verifying my description; a large room with vaulted ceiling, enormous fireplace and pieces of broken furniture scattered on the floor. The place looked like a junkyard.

"We're not the first, let's work our way over there; hold it, give me a hand with this door."

Pushing hard we worked the door into the frame and walked to the fireplace. Gathering bits of wood we started a fire, adding larger scrap wood until the blaze filled the hearth.

"Pure luxury, time for rest and recuperation. Let's build a nest, clear a place here by the hearth and we'll lay down that piece of rug. I see two sides of a wooden chair, we'll use them for backrests."

A loud banging from somewhere above held us still, eyes locked together.

"Don't like it, Jim."

"Neither do I, don't know what it is, but no enemy would announce himself?"

"Something up there, Jim, for sure it's not mice."

"So, we've ruled out the mice, how about something ordinary like wind slamming a door?"

"I want it to be the wind slamming a door, there's not much that's happened to me since I got off a landing barge and jumped in water up to my chin that's been ordinary."

"Let's have a nip, toast some thick slices of homemade bread, heat chunks of cheese and pork belly fat, load up the fire then sit here and enjoy our good fortune. How does that hit you?"

"Know what I think?"

"Don't keep me waiting."

"I think one day you'll tell the story of the haunted castle on a mountain top in Hungary where you stayed one night to get warm and a giant, wearing clinking armor, clumped down the stairs with a two edged sword held over his head and chased you out and down the road; the last thing you saw, he was closing the gate."

I sat silent, bread in one hand, cheese in the other, smiling and shaking my head.

"Astounding, just like that, I won't add a word."

"You might, the night's got a long way to go."

"Know something?"

"What's that?"

"I kind of hope there's something to add."

"Fifteen hundred friendlies and I got you, how's that for the luck of the draw?"

"Not bad, you hit the jackpot."

Conversation lagged with my rejoinder. We sharpened the end of two back rails from a chair, speared slices of bread on one, cheese and fat on the other and held them over red embers at the sides of the fire until they smoked then sat down and devoured our feast.

Poking the fire with a long stick, I spread embers across the hearth, loaded it with heavy pieces and stretched out in a half-sitting position and closed my eyes.

"What happened in Alaska? You didn't finish, haven't you made it up yet?"

"Let me see, where was I?"

"You were aiming a fire hose at the sentiment dirt on the other side of Prunella Creek."

"That was a remarkable day, it was Esther, not Prunella and sediment, not sentiment. Go back to school, Pat, reading and writing will be a big help filling out forms."

"What forms?"

"There are forms for everything – applications, income tax."

"What's that?"

"I won't spoil your day."

"Never mind that, what did you find?"

"I found an elephant."

A long moment of silence followed, then Pat erupted.

"Son-of-a-bitch, you really are a basket case, no question, when you get home they'll slam you on the funny farm and throw the key away. What the hell do you mean, you found an elephant?"

"Last warning, if you interrupt, no more story."

"Let's have it."

"I washed out a tusk, half a circle, taller than you, which isn't saying much. We moved it to the bunkhouse and leaned it against the outside wall in the shade. It was a monster, blue, in perfect condition. Next, I washed a piece of meat you couldn't lift off the ground if you went into training. One side was covered with hair. University of Alaska geologist came out later that night around eleven, my stuff blew his mind."

"What the hell could he see in the middle of the night?"

"Ever hear of the midnight sun? Twenty-one June, the sun shines for twenty-four hours, give or take a few minutes. Incidentally, it wasn't from an elephant, it was from a mastodon, a distant cousin, mammutidae, that's Latin for mastodon; don't struggle with it, call it an elephant. Can you handle that?"

"Screw you, what happened to the tusk and the prime rib?"

"Gave it to the University, he took it in that night, said the sun would destroy it; if it dried too fast, it would turn to dust."

A frightening sound like giant wings flapping came from somewhere in the wide corridor that ran into the wing near the stairway. We sat up motionless, waiting.

"Let's get the hell out of here."

"Weird, Pat, that was man made, go to sleep, I'll take the watch and keep the fire burning."

"Fat chance, sleep in a madhouse? No way."

We dozed off, wakened time and again by banging and scuffling sounds, screaming noises and strong drafts that caused the fire to flare, sending out ashes and sparks. By first light Pat was on his feet.

"That's it, let's go."

"Those were night noises, Pat, get smart, there's a logical explanation for everything."

"Give me one."

"It was the brandy, maybe fatigue, we've pushed ourselves to the limit, we're hallucinating or we have invaded someone's domicile."

"At the same time, you're pushing me to the limit, buddy."

"Let's have some food. How about toast and cheese with pork belly fat?"

"Don't know how I'd get along without you, but I'd like to try. Nothing you say makes sense – are you all right?"

"Not really, think about it, last night, alone, without me, you would've been on your knees praying."

"I don't know how."

"Times like that it'll come, take my word for it."

The toast and cheese got us going and when the sun rose over the horizon we hit the road. Halfway down the hill we stopped and turned back to face the castle.

"He can have it, Jim."

"Who can?"

"Count Dracula."

"He deserves it. Let's move, we're going to get out of this never, never land, Pat, any day now."

CHAPTER XXVIII

Persistence, coming from our lack of options, moved us after dark into Cluj, Romania. We followed a main thoroughfare with three and four story buildings that suggested we were finally in a city.

A full moon revealed an absence of debris. Entranceways were well kept and lights here and there at different levels indicated the neighborhood was residential. A church spire became our 'guide on' as we walked the center of the road.

"There's our target, my school years tell me there's a rectory next door. Know what that means?"

As usual, Teel asked, "Why don't you tell me?"

"It means food, maybe a shower and a bed and answers to our questions. How does that hit you?"

"Let's go find it."

"Pray it's Catholic."

"Why Catholic?"

"Knowledge, my friend, that's their secret."

A two-story residential structure beside the church showed light in several upstairs windows and from a mail drop on the left side of the large door.

I knocked, waited, closed my fist and hammered. The answer was a single word, not understood.

I shouted, "American, USA, soldiers, American."

Sounds of someone working the hardware held us silent, then the door opened a crack.

"Where is home?"

"United States, America, we were German prisoners, we escaped."

There was the sound of voices and the door was opened just enough to permit entrance.

"Come."

Teel followed me through the opening. A domestic closed and secured the door as another man standing farther back asked identification.

I held out my wrist and pulled back my sleeve, pronouncing each syllable separately.

"My U.S. Army identification, name James J. Hannon, U.S. Army Serial Number 0300319."

The man motioned us to follow, turned into a smaller hall and stopped, raised his hand, opened the door and entered. Conversation followed, overheard but not understood, then a smiling Priest wearing a black suit came to the door and put out his hand.

"English, a little, come." He led us into a well-furnished, small dining room.

"Padre Antiscue, religion?"

I answered, "Jesuit."

"Bless you."

I bumped Teel and whispered, "Call him Father."

"Sit please." The Priest walked into the kitchen.

"We hit the jackpot, you've been taking those smart pills again"

"The magic word, buddy, was Jesuit."

"I thought you said Catholic."

"The Catholic Church has many religious orders. Society of Jesus is one, Jesuit for short. My school was Jesuit."

Father Antiscue approached carrying two steaming mugs, sat them in front of us and sat down.

"Eggs, bacon now."

Teel leaned back in his chair and raised his hands. "Wake me, I must be dreaming."

"Soon you are home. There is something, after dinner, we visit an important man close by."

The domestic came through the door carrying two plates, put them down and stepped back.

Teel stared at his plate and whispered, "My God, sorry Father, this is unbelievable."

The plates were loaded with fried eggs, bacon and toast.

"Lieutenants, now you will face your vow to God. German people suffer much, forgive them in the name of Jesus Christ."

Silence followed Father Antiscue's solemn reminder. He waited, and then said, "Love them for they too are God's children."

I looked at the Priest. "Do you know a place called Maidonek?"

Antiscue shook his head.

"A death camp, Germans exterminated men, women and children there, most of their victims were Jews."

"Lieutenant, many people were killed in Russia, temporal affairs are not my province. I am devoted to spiritual matters, what you have seen is secular, transitory, temporary. Life to come will be eternal, forever.

He stood up and smiled. "When you have finished, I will take you for a short visit."

When he left the room Teel leaned on the table, lit a cigarette and said, "It never happened, get used to it."

"It happened, we're still alive. It'll take some doing to love those murderous bastards. Let's not keep Father Antiscue waiting."

The Oradea Mansion was a new experience for us. We followed the Priest up a wide stairway rising out of a spectacular three-story foyer, followed a wide corridor covered with oriental carpets, wall hangings, paintings and tapestries, into a paneled room.

Two lovely young ladies sat on a divan at the end of a heavy, ornate table. Baron Oradea was standing on the far side of the table. Slender and elderly, his austere manner set the mood.

Father Antiscue and Oradea spoke in their native tongue, then the Baron addressed us.

"Please, sit, be comfortable, it is my good fortune to meet Americans."

There was no hand shaking or amenity offered. I felt it would be a short visit.

We sat opposite the Baron; Teel offered Lucky Strikes. Oradea held his between thumb and forefinger, palm up; his delicate manner with the business of smoking did not go unnoticed.

"Remarkable, I have not forgotten the unique quality of your cigarettes. America does many things well and some not so well."

He studied Teel then turned to me. "Where were you held?"

"Midway between Danzig and Posen, a permanent prison camp for American ground officers."

"You were treated well?"

I waited, sensing something strange was emerging in that immaculate parlor.

"We were prisoners, sir."

"The propaganda that has been issued concerning German abused prisoners was not present, is that so?"

"I'm not familiar with the propaganda."

"Death camps, gas chambers, that propaganda."

I looked at Father Antiscue who was smiling, concentrating on the ceiling.

"Maidonek."

I waited. Oradea raised his cigarette, "Maidonek, what is that?"

"Gas chambers, a death camp."

"Do you believe that, Lieutenant?"

"I was there."

Oradea engaged Father Antiscue in a brief monologue, then turned back.

"The cunning Churchill and the barbarian Stalin have filled your President with self-serving information designed to hold the Germans responsible for the great war and the chaos that will come after."

He smoked for a moment, then carefully tapped the ash into a tray.

"Now will come the final days. Germany will surrender. The overwhelming combination of America's industrial capacity, largely funded by international Jewish bankers, is the difference between the warring nations. The same financial power that denied assistance to a depleted Germany after World War One."

Again he conferred at length with the Priest who nodded and smiled.

"Are you aware, Lieutenant, of your President's heritage?"

"Dutch, I believe."

"President Roosevelt or Rosenfeld, as it was in the beginning, is a Jew. Does that change your view?"

"Should it?"

My answer brought the first crack in Oradea's polished veneer. He crushed his cigarette in the tray, placed both hands on the table and raised his voice.

"Remember what I say; you will need the German's unrivaled military strength when you are at war with Russia, and then,

Lieutenants, as they say in America, 'the shoe will be on the other foot'."

Antiscue, reading the signal, got to his feet. "Thank you. As always, your hospitality is much appreciated. Lieutenants, we go now."

The girls sat unmoving, indifferent to the visitor's departure.

We walked in silence to the rectory where the Priest escorted us to an unoccupied dormitory.

"Sleep well. My duties tomorrow, early mass and other matters, I will say goodbye now."

We undressed and crawled into bed.

"Reminds me, want to hear another story? When I was a kid, in our Jesuit school we had a Sister Superior in charge of all household matters and meals, we called her Attila the Nun…"

Teel's loud snores interrupted.

"That's one way to put him to sleep. So, the good Father had a purpose, we are to carry the Baron's message to our Jewish President, who buried Hitler's master race and will do the same to Emperor Hirohito."

I turned over and closed my eyes.

CHAPTER XXIX

Mid-morning we got up; speaking in whispers, walked into the corridor and stopped. The absence of any sound was unbroken as we walked to the door and slipped out.

Teel looked back over his shoulder. "Good luck to Father Antscrew."

"It's Antiscue, as a kid, you probably liked dirty words."

"Didn't you?"

"Look ahead, traffic on that cross street."

Picking up the pace, we reached the cross street and turned right into a wide-open public place that held an enormous crowd gathered in front of a multi-storied building with columns marking its front.

"Looks official, maybe the City Hall."

Teel started walking, then shouted, "Come on, we'll get some answers, let's get there before it disappears."

We pushed through until Russian soldiers with lowered rifles stopped us. Three Jeeps with white stars and USAAF painted on the hood held us speechless for a moment – then we shouted and struggled to get through the line as a group of U.S. and Russian uniforms emerged from the entrance.

I held up my hand, shouting and waving.

"Colonel, U.S. soldiers, Jim Hannon, Pat Teel, we escaped from a German Prison Camp – we're Americans!"

The Colonel stared, moved closer.

"Let them through."

As we broke through, the Colonel embraced me and a Captain put his arms around Teel who was still shouting.

"I was in Colonel Darby's Rangers, sacked at Anzio, look at my shoulder patch."

The Captain smiled, "O.K., O.K., we believe you. Is that your dress uniform?"

Everyone laughed.

"I'm Colonel McCrary, this is Captain Swenson, where the hell did you come from?"

"Lieutenant Jim Hannon, 509th Parachute Battalion, prison camp in Poland near Danzig. Taken prisoner at Anzio, we've been on the loose since January."

McCrary shouted, "He's real, General, both of them; that's General Mc Narney, 12th Air Force."

"I can't believe it, Cluj, Rumania, we lucked out. We were on our way to Budapest, Colonel."

McCrary turned to the General, "General McNarney, Lieutenant Hannon and Lieutenant Teel, escaped P.O.W.'s."

The General returned our salute and said, "Let's go back inside."

He spoke to the Russian Officers, entered the building and led the way to the dining room where a long table was loaded with wine, Vodka and banquet food. When we were seated, McNarney rapped the table.

"Tell me about your route, name cities or places. Who's the spokesman?"

Teel turned and put his hand on my shoulder. "Here's the man with the words."

After taking a long drink of water, I responded.

"We were in the U.S. Ground Officer's camp in Schubin, Poland, Oflag 64, between Posen and Danzig. January twenty-one Germans were moving prisoners into Germany. Teel and I got away, decided to go east."

Colonel McCrary interrupted, "You can write in detail later, give the General your major stops and routes."

I nodded and continued, "Posen, Kutno, then Warsaw, they call it Varshava, crossed the Vistula on ice, bridge was down, Praga, full of refugees, Rembertov, the Polygon, a refugee camp, Deblin, Lublin, went through Maidonek, a death camp on the Lublin Chelms Highway, walked, hitched rides, climbed aboard trains, caught Russian Army trucks to Jaroswow, then to Pryzsmsl…"

Colonel McCrary was making notes. He turned to me. "Hold it, what was that, spell it please?"

"P R Y Z S M S L."

General McNarney smiled, "If you can pronounce that, you're more than a linguist, move along, time is short."

I continued, "Dukla, through Dukla Pass, Metzilaborce, Czechoslovakia, Miskoch, Hungary and then, thank God, Cluj, Rumania."

"Did you encounter Germans?"

"We did, our luck held, we got through."

The General pushed his chair back. "Lieutenant, both of you, I want you to know the importance of your report. Tell it like it happened, a world we know little about, a rare view indeed. Again, I commend you for your power of observation. Captain Swenson, they're in your hands."

Hand shaking and compliments came from all sides until we boarded Swenson's Jeep and drove to the airfield. After a long wait in late afternoon we boarded a C-47, bucket seats lining each side faced inward.

When we were settled at cruising altitude, I fastened my eyes on the man opposite wearing British battle dress with rank of Captain. He projected a strange, withdrawn manner, a big man, broad shouldered with a fighter's face, short blond hair and large hands resting on his knees. He had no fingernails and no ears.

I nodded, the Captain's eyes were fixed on me, a hard, unnerving stare; he didn't return the greeting. An American Air Force Lieutenant sat on the Britisher's left side; a slender, dark haired man in perpetual motion, wild eyed, talking constantly in a low voice – he would not make eye contact.

Teel leaned close and whispered, "Are you thinking what I'm thinking?"

"Not now, button up."

Forty minutes from setting down. I went to the restroom. When I came out, Captain Swenson was waiting.

"It's over, short time now, Jim."

"Any minute I'll wake up. The Captain and Lieutenant across from me, tell me about them."

Swenson shook his head. "The Captain was picked up by the Gestapo, they pulled his fingernails, cut off his ears and other things. He's in his own world. Lieutenant was a B-17 co-pilot; Ploesti flak took the pilot's head off. With power gone, the Lieutenant took it down, crash landed; he was so drenched in blood they couldn't

189

recognize his uniform. He's what's known as a Section 8. He lost it, Jim. Incidentally, those other people are their keepers."

We stretched our legs and laid our heads on the backrest.

"There's one still living his blood bath and the other can't find his way back. I hope we're normal."

"There's no such thing, Jim. I've thought about it, normal is 'Dullsville', people want everybody to disconnect their minds and become zombies like themselves."

"Dullsville, Pat, is where we might be until they put an end to our military career. I have one thing on my mind, Ginger, a full tank of gas and then the highway – Lake Tahoe, Yosemite, Laguna Beach, whatever fits our mood."

"I have two things on my mind, Gen and Pat Junior going on two. Don't know if it will work, you know my history, never had a family. Walked out of the orphanage when I was fourteen, first fight the day after my sixteenth birthday, never fought amateur, four rounds in Newark, New Jersey, took a real stomping. I put him down twice and then it was his turn and he knew what to do with it."

"Are you going to try again?"

"I don't really know, it's a hard way to make a living."

"I gave it a show, Pat, won them all until the last one, eight rounds, something exploded inside my skull in the third, came to in my corner after the bell, nothing in between. I got a decision and hung them up, carried a permanent headache for a year. You said it, it's a tough way to make a living."

In the twilight and silence I turned to the window and closed my eyes while the force grew. An uncommon warm feeling held me; our good fortune might be a dream.

I opened my eyes as it came to me, a turn in the road, U.S. Air Force Jeeps, General McNarney, a curtain dropped on fear, pain, loneliness, the ugliness. "How it might have been," I whispered.

"A roll of the dice, the hard way."

The crackle of the intercom stopped my journey down the long corridor – a cold, gray morning, climbing the gangplank in Newport News, Virginia and then the great circle ending in Naples.

"Pilot here, we'll be at the gate fifteen, sixteen minutes, fasten your seat belts."

Captain Swenson entered from the flight deck and sat down. "A few thoughts, Jim, curiosity, the bad part, how was it?"

Just then the throttle eased back. From across the aisle a plaintive wail rose, held and slowly faded.

"A walk in the park, Captain."

FINIS

About the Author

A summary of my World War II service is listed below with mention of other related incidents.

My enlistment in the United States Army occurred on 9 May 1942 with an Honorable Discharge 30 March 1946.

In addition, I hold an Honorable Discharge from the United States Navy and the Royal Canadian Air Force.

I served on active duty in Morocco. No. Africa, Italy and China. Awards include: Parachute Wings, Combat Infantryman's Medal, European Campaign Medal with two Battle Stars, Prisoner of War Medal, China-Burma Indian Campaign Medal with one Battle Star, Soldier's Medal, Breast Order of Yun Hui, Presidential Citation, purple Heart with cluster and a U.S. Army Intelligence College Certificate.

Became a German Prisoner of War, Anzio, Italy 29 February 1944, held in Cina Cita, Rome/Latterina, Florence/ Dachau, Munich/ Schubin, Poland - Oflag 64. I escaped 21 January 1945, made my way across Poland, Czechoslovakia, Hungary, rescued in Cluj Romania by General McNarney 12 March 1945.

Arrived Washington, D.C. 20 March 1945, interrogated and de-briefed, had one on one meetings with General George C. Marshall, who changed my M.O. to Military Intelligence, Secretary of War Stimson, Mrs. George Patton and others. Chief of Intelligence requested I go to China-Burma-India Theater.

Appointed member of an Intelligence Service located in Hunan Province, China. Arrived Kunming 11 June 1945; performed several missions including the parachute rescue of a critically wounded U.S. fighter pilot. Other activity and final mission was as member of a six-man team. Parachuted into a cornfield opposite the entrance to a Japanese Prison Camp, 700 miles behind Japanese lines. Affected the rescue of 1500 Allied men, women and children. Escorted ex-prisoners by rail to Tsingtao and Army Transport to Shanghai. Returned to U.S. 19 November 1945.

APPENDIX

A copy of a printed book, 'Majdanku', translation Maidonek, was given to me by Basiz Zygmunt, a man who gave me a hot meal and shelter for the night in the town of Lublin.

Basiz pointed across the valley and said, "Maidonek – death camp – more than a million people went up that stack and floated down everywhere – black snowflakes contaminated the air, the streets, public places, school yards, church yards, markets, our homes, our clothes, our minds – one day, translate this book into English."

That 'one day' came 57 years later in May of 2002. The pictures are also from this book, 'Oboz W Majdanku' described in my Chronicle, *FIVE MARKS*.

I was there, February 1945, overwhelmed by the ghastly slaughter house just as the German's left it in the month of August 1944 described in detail in *FIVE MARKS*

James Jess Hannon

BORYS GORBATOW

THE CONCENTRATION CAMP AT MAJDANEK

(Obóz w Majdaku)

FOREIGN LANGUAGE PUBLISHING HOUSE
MOSCOW 1944

DECLARATION
BY GERMAN GENERAL MOSER
TO THE RED ARMY COMMAND

Lieutenant General Moser,
Former commandant of the
372nd Field Command in Lublin

DECLARATION

I, *Hilmar Moser*, was born in the year 1880 in the town of Langenorla (Rosa district). I have served in the Germany army since 1902. I was promoted to the rank of major general in 1935, and that of lieutenant general in 1942. I have been recipient of all German decorations and awards for service in combat.

For 42 years I have been a conscientious soldier, I have taken part in two world wars, and have been seriously wounded.

I have no reason to gloss over or cover up the monstrous crimes of Hitler, I consider it my duty to tell the whole truth about the "extermination camp" built by the Hitlerites near Lublin, along the Chelm highway.

At the end of November 1942 I arrived in Lublin as commandant of the 372nd Field Command.

My predecessor, General von *Altrock*, along with his field command, was transferred about three weeks later to the East. In briefing me about his duties, he informed me that there was a concentration camp at Lublin run by the SD[1]. He started that according to military regulations, the commandant of a field command, being a representative of the Armed Forces, was strictly prohibited from visiting the camp or inquiring about what went on there.

Shortly thereafter, General of the Infantry *Heinicke*, commandant of the Military District of the General Government[22] arrived in Lublin; the field command was directly under his jurisdiction.

---

[1] Translation's note: SD—*Sicherheitsdienst – Security Police*
[2] Translator's note: Official name given to German-occupied Poland

He repeated the regulations that Gen. Altrock had told me about, and reiterated the strict prohibition against concerning myself with what was happening in the concentration camp.

Among other things, he told me. "What's going on there is like molten iron—you don't want to touch it!"

In the first phase of my tenure I made every effort to familiarize myself with the area under my jurisdiction. Later I attempted to gather factual information about the concentration camp. I learned the following:

The camp extended several kilometers along the Chelm highway and several kilometers into the adjacent terrain. I estimate it covered about 30 square kilometers. Some direct railways spurs led from the main RR station to the camp. On the outside it was surrounded by an ordinary barbed wire fence, with a guard house a short distance inside.

I don't know when the camp was built; I don know that while I was in Lublin it expanded considerably.

On one occasion, while inspecting potential sites for construction of the "Lublin Defense Zone" fortifications, positions that ran along the east wall of the concentration camp (outside the enclosure), I was also about 30 meters inside the camp enclosure with some other officers, who were in charge of the construction project.

I had no intention of visiting the camp itself, which, as I mentioned before, was strictly off-limits for the reasons stated above.

Nonetheless I found out a great deal about what went on there.

Everybody in Lublin called it the "concentration camp" or the "Jewish camp," since in the beginning its inmates were mostly Jews; later there were representatives of a wide range of nationalities, so-called political criminals, including Germans.

During the winter of 1943-44 a large number of prisoners were put to death there, including, I was appalled to learn, many women and children.

The number of deaths reached the hundreds of thousands.

The victims were either shot or gassed to death.

More than once I was also told that the condemned were forced to do extremely arduous work, depleating their strength, and that as they worked they were severely beaten.

I was also appalled to learn that the victims were tormented and physically tortured before being put to death.

In the spring of that year a large number of bodies were exhumed and burned in specially built ovens, clearly to erase any trace of crimes committed on Hitler's orders.

The huge ovens were built of bricks and iron; they constituted a large-capacity crematorium. The stench of death drifted into the town from the east, so that even the poorly informed citizenry knew what was happening in that horrible place.

I obtained information about the dreadful camp through conversations with the following persons; General von *Altrock*—my predecessor, commandant of the field command; General *Renner*, former commander of the 174th Reserve Division in Lublin; Major *Gleisner*, commander of the 991st Landwehr Rifle Battalion; Doctor *Klaus* and *Osor*, chiefs of the Regional Provisions and Farm Resources Group, and Major *Hartmann*, who for five years was my adjutant and confidential aide.

I personally asked Major *Hartmann* to find out what was happening in the camp, and he provided me with detailed information.

The most compelling validation of the information I received was the foul odor that I myself was so often witness to.

I have no words to express my revulsion at these incredible atrocities and I believe that any decent German should renounce a government capable of ordering such organized mass murder.

Evidence that the operations of the extermination camp were directed by. Hitler's authorities can be drawn from the fact that Himmler himself visited the camp when he came to Lublin in the summer of 1943.

I consider it my duty—as a general and a soldier with 42 years in the army, a combat veteran of two world wars, a survivor of serious injuries, and the last commandant of the Lublin district field command—to cooperate in bringing to full light all the atrocities that were perpetrated in the concentration camp. I call upon all members of the military forces under me in Lublin to gather together information on all the crimes they know about that took place in the Lublin extermination camp.

Lt. Gen. [Hilmar] Moser

August 29, 1944

THE POLISH-SOVIET COMMISSION ON MAJDANEK

(*Polpress* communiqué)

Near Lublin in the Majdanek extermination camp the German occupiers perpetrated the mass murder of Soviet prisoners and Poles, French, Czechs, Jews, Belgians, Hungarians, Serbs, Greeks and immates f other European nationalities.

In view of the fact that the Germans carried out mass murders of Soviet prisoners in that camp, the Polish Committee for National Liberation approached the Soviet government with a proposal to create an Extraordinary Polish-Soviet Investigative Commission to investigate the German crimes in Lublin and to appoint its representatives to the Commission: Prof. M. Graschenko, Prof. Prozorovski and Prof. D. Kudriavtsev.

The Extraordinary Polish-Soviet Commission was headed by Mr. Witos, vice chairman of the Polish Committee for National Liberation. The members of the Comission—Rev. Dr. Druszyński, Prof. Bialkowski, prosecuting Magistrate Balcerzak of the Appeals Court, Prof. Of Forensic Medicine Szyling-Synagalewiez, and a representative of the Polish Committee for National Liberation, Dr. Sommerstein (Poland), Prof. Graschenko, Prof. Prozorovski and Prof. Kudriavtsev (USSR) — proceeded to investigate the German fascist crimes in Lublin with the aim of identifying and disclosing the names of the organizers and direct perpetrators of said crimes.

Lublin, August 17, 1944.
Reczpospolita

THE CONCENTRATION CAMP AT MAJDANEK

1

When the wind blew from the direction of Majdanek, the citizens of Lublin closed their windows. The wind brought a foul odor to the town. You couldn't breathe. You couldn't eat. You couldn't live.

The wind blew from Majdanek and filled the people with fear. Black, foul smoke poured steadily from the smokestack of the camp's crematorium. The wind carried the smoke to the town. The heavy stench of death hung over the people of Lublin. There was no way to escape it.

The Poles called the Majdanek crematorium "The devil's ovens" and the camp was known as the "death factory."

The Germans showed no restraint in occupied Poland. They wanted the Poles to smell death every day, because fear helps control rebellious spirits. All of Lublin knew about the "death factory." All of Lublin knew that in the Krebecki forest Russian prisoners of war and Poles from Lublin Castle were being shot. Everyone saw the trainloads of doomed victims being brought here, to the camp, from very country in Europe.

Everyone knew the fate that awaited them—the gas chamber and the oven.

The wind from Majdanek tapped on the windowpanes, "Poles, think about the devil's ovens, think about death! Remember that there is no life for you—there is only insert existence, impermanent and desolate. Remember you are merely raw material for the devil's ovens. Remember, and tremble!"

The foul odor hung over Lublin. The foul odor hung over Poland. The foul odor hung over all of a Europe tortured by Hitler's henchmen.

The foul odor was the weapon with which the Germans planned to suffocate humanity and rule the world.

2

"Dachau No. 2" was what the Germans first called the SS forces' concentration camp at Lublin. Both in terms of magnitude and operations, the "death factory" at Majdanek far outstripped the horrors of Dachau.

We found ex-prisoners of Dachau, Buchenwald and Auschwitz there.

"Things are much worse here!," they said, "*Much* worse...!"

The death factory covered twenty-five square kilometers with all its facilities: prison yards or compounds, spaces between them, gas chambers, crematoriums, trenches where shootings took place, gallows for hangings, and a brothel for the German camp guards.

The camp is located to kilometers from Lublin, close to the Lublin-Chelm highway. In the distance you can see its guard towers. The barracks are all identical—lines up with mathematical precision. Each is clearly marked with a distinctive "address" placard. All together they form a yard (called a "field"). There are six "fields" in the camp, and each is its own world, separated from the neighboring world by barbed wire fencing. In the center of each field was a prominently positioned gallows, used for public executions. All the roads in the camp are paved; the grassy areas are well manicured. In front of the German administration buildings there are flowerbeds and wicker lawn chairs for relaxation in the bosom of nature.

In the camp there are workshops, storerooms, a water plant and an electric lighting plant. One facility was used to store canisters of "Zyklon" for the gas chambers. There were yellow labels on the canisters: "Special—for Eastern Areas" and "To be opened by trained personnel only." There is a shop where they made clothes hangers. The hangers bore the SS insignia. They were distributed to the prisoners before entering the gas chamber. The victims themselves had to put their clothes on the hangers.

Cabbages grew profusely in the camp's yards. Plump and inviting. But they were inedible. They were nourished by blood and ashes. The Germans strewed the ashes of the crematorium victims over the yards. Their gardens were fertilized by human ashes.

The whole camp gives the impression of an immense factory or a large industrialized farm. But for the foul odor, even the crematorium ovens have the appearance of small electrical smelting furnaces. The German company that produced the ovens designed them with a look to the future by mounting serpentine coils onto the pipe to proved a constant supply of free hot water.

Thus the factory, which seems inconceivable, but which existed in reality, was a death factory. A death mill. Everything here, from the quarantine facilities to the crematorium, was designed for the annihilation of human beings—designed with rule and compass, blueprinted and discussed with German physicians and engineers as if the projected facility were a slaughterhouse.

The Germans did not succeed in destroying the camp when they retreated. They were only able to burn the crematorium building, but the ovens themselves remained intact. A table on which the murderers stripped and robbed their victims also survived. Half-carbonized skeletons were also preserved in the "corpse dump." To this day a nauseating odor of burnt human flesh permeates the crematorium.

The entire camp has been preserved. The gas chambers. The barracks. The storerooms. The gallows. Barbed were entanglements with alarm systems, dog paths. Even the dogs, Germans shepherds, were left behind. They stare warily from their kennels, perhaps bored by the inactivity. They now have no one to attack and mutilate.

Some prisoners managed to evade the hands of the murderers. There are witnesses, many witnesses. And some of the murderers were caught.

We spoke to them all.

"I lived through it!" says a rescued prisoner, who himself does not understand how he survived.

"I saw it!" says a witness who himself does not understand why what he saw didn't drive him insane.

"We did it," say the murderers blankly.

Every word of what we're about to relate can be confirmed by documents and testimony of witnesses and of the Germans themselves.

Finally we can rip the veil off Majdanek and reveal to the whole world the story of Lublin's "extermination camp."

3

Extermination camp. *Vernichtungslager.*
International death camp.

Over its gates might well have been emblazoned "Abandon all hope, ye who enter here. Ye shall never return."

Trainloads of doomed prisoners arrived here from all parts of occupied Europe. From occupied areas of Russia and Poland, from France, Belgium and Holland, from Greece, Yugoslavia and Czechoslovakia, from Austria and Italy, from other German concentration camps, from the Warsaw and Lublin ghettos. To be annihilated.

Here, in the remote eastern corner of Poland, it was possible to do the things that the Germans might have found difficult to do in the West. Here they finally put to death all who had managed to endure and survive the hard-labor regimes of Dachau and Flossenburg. Anyone who was still alive, who breathed and could crawl, but could no longer work. Anyone who opposed the invaders. Anyone sentenced to death by the Germans. People of many different nationalities and ages—men, women and children. Poles, Russians, Jews, Ukrainians, Byelorussians, Lithuanians, Latvians, Italians, French, Albanians, Croatians, Serbs, Czechs, Norwegians, Germans, Greeks, Dutch, Belgians, Greek women with shaved heads, with numbers tattooed on their arms. Blind martyrs of the underground "Dora" factory where the "V-1" missiles were made. Political prisoners from German camps with red triangles on their backs, ex-convicts with green, "saboteurs" with black, sectarians with purple, Jews with yellow. Children—from babes in arms to adolescents. Those under 8 were put together with their parents. Eight-year-olds and even "delinquents" were assigned to common barracks. Children reached adulthood very early in the German death camps.

How many hundreds of thousands were murdered in that international death camp? It is hard to say. The ashes of the cremated victims were scattered over the fields and the neighboring countryside by the wind.

But a terrible reminder remained.

Behind the crematorium there is an enormous storehouse. Heaped to overflowing with shoes—squashed, crumpled, compacted into piles—hundreds of thousands of shoes, boots and slippers.

The victims' footwear.

Tiny baby shoes with red and green tassels. High-fashion women's shoes. Ordinary kneeboots, warm old women's boots.

Footwear of people of different ages, wealth, social status, nationality. Stylish Parisian women's shoes beside the boots of a Ukrainian peasant. Death leveled them all. The owners of this footwear were similarly packed into a common grave to die.

It is appalling to look at those piles of shoes. They were all once worn by human beings. They walked on the earth. They trod the grass. They knew the boundless sky was above their heads. They breathed, worked, loved, dreamed... They were born for happiness as birds are born to fly.

Why did they become victims of this unspeakable tragedy? Why did death cut them down? Suddenly they're gone... The wind had dispersed their ashes... Only dead shoes, crumpled and torn, cry out, as only dead objects can...

What motivated the Germans to keep these dreadful souvenirs? Why did they collect and preserve them here?

We found the answer in a remote corner of a barrack. Collected there were stacks of shoe parts: soles, heels, uppers. All neatly sorted with German precision. All neatly separated into lots.

They were all bound for Germany.

Like ashes over the countryside, like the heat from the crematoriums to the coils. Blood on shoe soles doesn't smell!

Only the Germans are capable of that!

4

The assistant administrator of the camp was an SS man named Tumann. Witnesses say that he was never without his huge German shepherd.

Germans love dogs.

They love to play with them, feed them, spar with them. They quickly find a common language with dogs. Crematorium chief Munfeld had a well-behaved little dog. The chief of the Russian POW compound amused himself playing around with a favorite mastiff.

SS man Tumann never missed a single shooting, not a single execution. He especially liked to take part in them himself. If a car headed to witness an execution was full, he would jump onto the footboard just to get there.

Crematorium chief Munfeld even lived in the crematorium. The foul odor that was stifling the entire city of Lublin didn't bother him a bit. He maintained that the smell of burnt bodies was pleasant.

Munfeld loved to joke with the prisoners.

Encountering them in the camp, he would inquire in a kindly voice, "Well, how are you, my friend? See you soon at my little oven?" Than, slapping the terrified victim on the shoulder, he would say, "Oh no, don't worry; I'll have the oven nice and warm for you."

The he would walk away, with his dog at his side.

Witness Stanisław Galan, from a nearby village, who, with his wagon, was mobilized for work in the camp, stated, "I myself saw *Oberscharführer*[*] Munfeld grab a four-year-old little boy, lay him on the ground, stepped with one foot onto the child's leg, holding it down, and then pulling the other leg so as to split the unfortunate child in two. This I saw with my own eyes; the child's innards spilled onto the floor…"

After tearing the child apart, Munfeld tossed him into the oven. Then he petted his little dog.

When Munfeld left the camp to take a new, highly responsible post, he didn't take his little dog with him. He bade him a fond farewell and tossed him into the oven. Even here he remained true to his nature.

SS Man Theo Schollin, whom we have captured, had a very modest job in the camp: he was in charge of the storehouse. It was he who took the clothing from newly arrived prisoners. Then he examined them stripped. He told them to open their mouths. He had a special pair of nickel pliers, with which he extracted any gold teeth he found.

Before the war Schollin worked in a slaughterhouse: he was a butcher. Called into the army, he was immediately released, because Germany needed workers in its slaughterhouses.

In 1942, however, he was re-drafted and assigned to this camp. Now they needed butchers here.

---

[*] Translator's note: There is no one-to-one equivalency between U.S. military ranks and those of WWII Germany. Chroniclers conventionally leave the names of these ranks in the original German. *Oberscharührer* was a rank roughly somewhat higher than 'Staff Sergeant.'

Schollin stands in front of us now and weeps. He was captured. An SS man's tears! How loathsome those tears are!

Schollin did not weep much in former days. The Germans in the camp at Majdanek loved to laugh and play practical jokes.

Here is one of their "great" practical jokes: An SS man would come up to a prisoner, any prisoner, and say, "I'm going to shoot you right now!"

The prisoner would pale, but readied himself for the bullet. The SS man slowly took aim, first at the victim's forehead, then heart, as if deciding the best target. Then he would snap, "Fire!" A shot rang out.

The prisoner's body shuddered, his eyes closed.

The prisoner was struck in the head. He lost consciousness and fell. He came to a few minutes later, however, and saw German faces staring down at him: the one who had "shot" him, and the one who, unseen, had struck him from behind with a club.

The SS men were laughing so hard they had tears in their eyes.

"You died," they shouted at their victim, "You died, and now you're in the Great Beyond. And guess what? WE are in the Great Beyond, too! We, the Germans! The SS!

5

Yes, Hitler's fiends were convinced that heaven and earth both belonged to them.

All they had to do was exterminate half the population of Europe. Burn them in a crematorium.

They built the Majdanek camp with tremendous effort and energy over a period of three years. That was the first stage of construction.

The camp was built by the prisoners. They drained the mud and dug the pits and trenches.

They knew that they were building their own prison. Barracks in which to perish. Tangled barbed wire to prevent their escape. Gallows on which to hang. A crematorium in which to burn. The German system: Those doomed to die dug their own graves!

The camp grew on the bones and blood of the prisoners. They died while working, they died in the barracks. In the winter they froze to death. They dropped from starvation.

Every day during evening roll call, they were lined up for inspection. Those who could hardly stand were ordered to lie down on the ground. They lay down. They knew that meant death. They could no longer get up.

They lay there in the field all night. In the morning the dead and the still-living were dragged away by hooks, either to the crematorium or to be burned on pyres, Hindu style—a layer of wood planks, then a layer of bodies, a layer of planks, a layer of bodies...

Hauling the bodies of the dead was the job of the other prisoners. Anyone who refused to do so was shot on the spot. Conversations were short here in this extermination camp. Here human life was cheaper than a bullet. They killed you here with iron rods.

Prisoners were also sent to work in the crematorium. Those whose minds had become dulled or broken were preferred for this job. They were given generous amounts of vodka—good long gulps. Drunk, muddled by the heavy stench of death, they bustled around the devil's ovens. They knew that within a month they, too, would make the trip to the oven. They were officially called "unreliable witnesses" by the Germans.

One way or another, sooner or later, they knew that the oven would devour them. There was no escaping from the camp. All they heard was "Hurry up! Move!" And they slaved at those cursed ovens, numbing their spirits with vodka.

Within a month all of them had been sent to the gas chamber and then... to the oven...

The insatiable ovens devoured everyone. The smoke poured out continually. In one day the five ovens incinerated 1400 bodies.

The Germans wanted to expand the camp. They dreamed of a gigantic death mill. If they had had their way they would have shoved all of Poland into the crematorium.

With a crushing assault, the Red Army put an end to the fiendish work of the cremation ovens.

The time had come for settling of accounts and retaliation.

6

Persons who entered the Majdanek camp ceased to be human beings. They became objects to be destroyed. They were robbed of their valuables, their clothing. They were robbed of their names. Each was issued a tin number tag on a wire collar, which they had to wear around their neck at all times, and a striped prisoner's uniform. On the jacket of the uniform was painted a read, black or yellow triangle and a letter indicating the prisoner's nationality, "P" for Pole, "F" for French. Nationality determined the relationship of the guards toward the prisoner. Prisoners could forget their own names in the camp, but the guards never let them forget that they were a "Slav pig," a "Polish ox," a "Russian swine" or a "Jew."

With their tin number tags around their necks, the wire collar digging into their skin, the prisoners moved along their agonizing journey from quarantine to the crematorium. The journey could be very short. Or it could drag out over long months—months of slow, agonizing death. But it always led to *Oberscharführer* Munfeld's devil's ovens.

There was no escape.

Some convicts, who had been sentenced to hard labor in Italian sulfur mines, were sent to the camp. It is said that those sulfur mines are the most terrible places on earth, but the Italian convicts had survived them. Then they were sent to the camp at Lublin. Here they died quickly. The machinery of the Majdanek death factory cranked relentlessly, ruthlessly, inexorably.

It started with the quarantine.

New arrivals had to go through quarantine in the infirmary barrack for contagious tuberculosis. The twenty days of "quarantine" was sufficient even for the very strongest. They became acutely infected and carried the disease out with them to the common barracks.

In the single month of March 1944, according to data from German documents in the camp office, 1,654 people died of tuberculosis. These included 67 Italians, a large number of Poles, Russians and Czechs, as well as Albanians, Yugoslavs, Greeks, Croatians, Slovenians, Serbs, Lithuanians and Latvians.

Tuberculosis was not treated in the camp. Here, instead of treatments there were beatings. But the camp infirmary was sparkling clean, especially for German press correspondents and photographers and for the constantly expected "international commissions" who, as it turned out, never came. On the doors were neatly printed signs such as "Pharmacy" and "Operating Room," even though there were not even the most basic medicines or rudimentary medical instruments in the camp.

On the other hand, these items were not really necessary. Among the prisoners the word was: Don't go to the infirmary. No one who went to the infirmary ever returned to the barrack.

If you wanted to prolong your life on this earth, you had to conceal any illness.

There was a medical scale in the infirmary. At times the prisoners were weighed. Germans love order. They very carefully recorded in a book: weight of an adult prisoner: 32 kilograms.

Thirty-two kilograms! This was the weight of the prisoner's bones wrapped in dry yellow skin.

The prisoners received a "soup" made of grass cut in the yard beside the barracks. With bitter humor, the Majdanek prisoners called the grass "vitamin SS."

More prisoners died of starvation than from tuberculosis. People dropped while working, and the SS men beat them with iron rods.

In their evening reports, the doctors did not mention the deaths that occurred during the day. The dead were not removed. The living lay on the same bed boards as the dead, even right next to them. The following day the living prisoners got the deceased's food rations.

7

A person imprisoned in the "extermination camp" could be killed by anyone belonging to the administration of the camp: potato patch supervisor Müller and the lowest-level prisoner crew foreman (*kapo*). The *kapo* competed with the SS men in terms of zeal. Killing prisoners was not considered a crime; on the contrary, it was proof of competence, it fell within the sphere of duty.

The SS men boasted in front of the Gestapo men about their heroic feats in the camp. The Gestapo men did the same thing.

Every SS man, every *kapo* had his own method of torture. One preferred to kick the victim in the throat with his boot, another liked to dance around on the victim's stomach. A thin, bony SS woman from the women's compound flogged women with a whip. She whipped them on their breasts, their genitals, their buttocks. Her whip struck their bodies with a lewd swishing sound. A sadistic psychopath, she flogged women to death.

Among the SS there were also lovers of cruel jokes. Some set dogs on the prisoners, other amused themselves at the pool. They forced the prisoners to jump into the water, and when they surfaced, they were struck over the head with a club. If the prisoner did not drown, he was ordered out of the water and to get dressed. He had to dress in three seconds. If not, it was jump into the water again, again a blow on the head, again three seconds to dress... And so on, until the victims either died in the pool or dressed in three seconds. Obviously, in most cases they died.

Władisław Skowronek, a wagon driver, reports, "I saw with my own eyes a German SS woman bring six children to the crematorium, two little boys and four little girls. They were tykes—four to eight years old. Munfeld, the chief of the crematorium, stripped them naked, shot them with his revolver and tossed them into the oven. I happened to see it because I was bringing some boards to the storeroom."

Reports Wiesław Stopywa, "I saw what they did to my friend Czesław Krzeczkowski. He was 42 years old and a powerful man. But he was not standing straight in the lineup, so a Gestapo man started to beat him. He kicked him in the stomach with his boot... then with a rod... Then he jumped up and down on his stomach... But Krzeczkowski was still alive. He was a strong man. The Gestapo man grabbed a rod with a sharpened end and plunged it into Krzeczkowski's throat, then tugged upward and ripped his face. Krzeczkowski was still alive... His whole body was twitching. They put him on a stretcher and took him to the crematorium.

Piotr Denisov reports, "I saw an SS man kill a prisoner. I'm an engineer from Lublin. I was working in the camp laying sewage pipes. This SS man was guarding prisoners. He was a young guy, 19 or 20. He had a delicate, girlish face. I would never have taken him for an SS man. He singled out a young, strong Jewish fellow and ordered him to lower his head. The fellow obeyed. Then the SS man started beating him on the neck with a club. The Jew fell down. "Take him away!" ordered the SS man. They dragged him away, face down... over the frozen ground. There was snow on the ground, and it was stained with a trail of blood. But the Jew was still alive. So the SS man took a 60-kilo section of concrete pipe and threw it onto the Jew's back. And again, and again. I heard the horrible cracking of bones... and a scream. I started to scream myself. I didn't want to watch, but I couldn't force my eyes away. The SS man walked over to the Jew, opened his eyelid with the club... dead. Then he lit up a cigarette. And he had such a sweet girlish face!

8

It's not difficult to kill a person. All you need is an iron club. But you can't exterminate humanity.

That was precisely the maniacal idea that drove Hitler. Exterminate all humanity that he didn't like—the unsubmissive, the great of spirit, the freedom-loving. Or at least exterminate everything human in occupied Europe.

In order to accomplish this massive assault on humanity, the Germans needed gigantic, mechanized death factory complexes like the Lublin camp.

It's impossible to kill millions of people with automatic pistols. You need an enormous complex of all possible means of extermination known to man.

This is exactly what they built at Majdanek—a mass-production death factory.

Victims were shot in the forest, in the trenches. They were flogged to death with whips. Attacked by dogs. Bludgeoned with clubs. Their skulls were crushed. They were drowned in water. Stuffed into trucks and gassed—Pack 'em tighter! Tighter! They died of starvation. They died of tuberculosis. They suffocated in gray concrete chambers, packed to the maximum. Two hundred fifty, three hundred—Pack 'em tighter! Asphyxiated by Zyklon. Poisoned by chlorine. Observed through peepholes as they twitched and shook in their death throes. A new gas chamber was built. Asphyxiated. Burned on pyres. Burned in the old crematorium. Forced one by one through the narrow doors. Stunned by an iron rod on the head. Tossed into an oven. The dead and the living. The unconscious. Cram as many into the oven as possible—Pack 'em tighter! Tighter! Bodies hacked to pieces. Watched through a blue windowpane as their bodies shriveled and incinerated. Killed singly. Killed in groups. Whole truckloads.

Eighteen thousand at a time. Thirty thousand at a time. Assemble groups of Poles from Radom, Jews from the Warsaw Ghetto, Jews from Lublin. Rush them through the camp. Surrounded by dogs and riflemen. Flogged with whips, Move! Move!

Long lines of Jews filed through the camp, to the fifth "field." Silently. In rows. Holding hands. Children clinging to their parents. Silently. Silently.—"Hurry up!" "Let's go! Move!" The Germans drove them on. The dogs barked. The whips hissed. The lines quickened their pace. The ones toward the end of the line pressed upon those in front. They ran. They stumbled. They fell. They lost their breath.

Suddenly all the loudspeakers in the camp began to blare. Lively foxtrots, tangos. The camp froze in terror. Everyone knew: today there will be large-scale executions. The tractor revved its engine. The rumba replaced the foxtrot.

In the fifth field the doomed prisoners undressed. Down to bare skin. Everybody. Men, women, children. They were forced over to the trenches. Move! Hurry up! They lay down in the trenches, body-to-body. Submissively. Resigned to their fate.—Tighter! Squeeze together!—shouted the Germans. The people squeezed close together. They became entangled with each other. Arms, legs, heads no longer belonged to anybody. They existed separately, crushed, broken. Smothered. On top of the first layer a second. Then a third. The loudspeaker blared foxtrots. The tractor started to rumble. The whole trench was now filled to the top with a living, pulsing, groaning human mass, screaming at their executioners. The SS men sprayed the trench with automatic gunfire.

And all five ovens in the crematorium opened their greedy jaws. They were frantically overworked. Day and night. Fourteen hundred bodies every 24 hours. Not enough! They crammed more bodies into the ovens. Instead of six, they stuffed in seven bodies at a time. The temperature was increased. 1500°C. Not enough! They accelerated the incineration process. 45 minutes, 30, 25. The bricks in the ovens began to deform under the incredible heat. The cast-iron baffles melted. The crematorium's smokestack ceaselessly spewed out its billows of ashes. The black stench of death permeated the camp.

The wind blew the foul odor over the entire surrounding area.

Was it possible to survive the death Camp?

Some sought death themselves, to shorten the terrible agony. They threw themselves against the electrified barbed wire and died, blackened and contorted.

Engineer Denisov told us of another case of voluntary death:

Two prisoners approached an SS man and asked to be hanged.

"Hang us!"

The SS man looked at them with surprise and smiled.

"Sure. Be glad to."

He tied a noose, put it around the neck of the first one, placed him near the trench, gave the ends of the rope to two helpers and, telling them to hold on tight, he struck the prisoner in the back of the knee. The prisoner fell into the trench, trembled a few times in the noose and expired.

Immediately the second prisoner walked up to the trench. He loosened his collar, put the noose around his neck, lunged forward and followed after the first prisoner.

On a barrack wall we found scribbled, "Vanya Ivanov tried to kill himself and failed, and it was his own fault." Someone else, as if responding to the first, wrote, "If one could only die in such a way that one's death would bring some good!"

Was it possible to escape from the camp?

We heard of the "mutiny of the shovels" and of the "escape of the eighteen." Both of these actions involved Russian prisoners, and what they illustrate most of all is the Soviet Russians' spirit of dedication to the struggle for freedom.

The "mutiny of the shovels" took place in the Krębecki forest, where a group of Russian POWs from the camp were working. Seventeen Russians killed the German guard with their shovels and escaped.

The "escape of the eighteen" happened later. It was preceded by an actual meeting in a barrack. Question: to try or not to try an escape. Eighteen opted to try, fifteen opted to stay.

The eighteen decided to flee during the night. Those who remained promised not to betray them, and did not. Throwing five blankets over the barbed wire entanglements (which were not yet electrified at that time), the prisoners climbed over them and escaped.

That same night the Germans took the remaining fifteen out of the barrack and shot them.

I know of one more case of an escape. It was a Jew from Lublin named Dawidson. He escaped at the moment when they were being taken out of the camp to work. He knew that if he tried to escape they would shoot him. But he also knew that they would shoot him if he didn't try to escape. He didn't have much of a choice. He took off running, expecting a bullet in the back of his head. But the bullets missed him. He got away.

A Polish family who knew him gave him shelter. For two years and thirty days—until our armies marched into Lublin—the Poles concealed the Jew in their attic and fed him. The entire two years and thirty days he crawled around so that no footsteps would betray him or the family that was concealing him. For the entire two years he never saw anyone, didn't talk to anyone. They brought food to him in the attic, and that was all. He forgot how to talk. He got used to no daylight. But he survived. We saw him.

And, just like him in his attic, thousands of people in the camp also lived with uncertain hope...

On a barrack wall in the camp we found a drawing made with a blue pencil. No signature. No words. The drawing was that of an ordinary Ukrainian landscape. How much bitter longing that picture held, for home, for freedom... how much hope!

Thus, even here in the death camp, people didn't lose hope... And they placed their hope in the Red Army.

And the Red Army didn't let them down.

10

Nowadays thousands of people from Lublin come to Majdanek. They come to look at the dreadful camp.

For three years it was a nightmare for them. For three years they had breathed in the foul odor of the camp's ovens. For five years they lived under the Germans' whip.

The death camp had been enveloped in foul stench and secrecy. Now there are no secrets. Here are the devil's ovens. Here are the trenches where the prisoners were shot. Here are the remains of the half-charred bodies in the crematorium.

The people look and do not weep. They have already wept all their tears—there are no more. The crowd cries out.

Germans are working in the trench. They were captured in the camp. The butchers have been ordered to dig up the bodies of their victims.

Their shovels strike the earth with a hollow sound. The Germans work silently. They merely tremble with fear at the furious shouts of the crowd and lower their heads toward their shovels.

The crowd cries out.

The shovels strike the ground. A woman screams in horror. A little child's foot protrudes out of the lumpy clay mass.

"Murderers!" the crowd shouts, "Murderers!"

They bring German captives, soldiers and officers, up to the site. There are over eighty of them. To protect them from the anger of the crowd, they are led to the other side of the trench. Their guards point to the work of their hands. The child's body is pulled out and lies beside the remains of others.

The Germans approach in silence. Some turn away. Others look at the body blankly.

"Bandits!" the crowd shouts, "Murderers!"

The crowd grows. From the highway, from the surrounding villages they come. Only the trench separates them from the butchers. In the trench amidst the remains of the victims is the body of a child.

The Germans walk with their heads down, their eyes to the ground. Their arms behind them. The crowd is furious. There is no hissing whip to scourge them as they shout, "Murderers! Degenerates! Sadists!"

An elderly Pole waves his cane above his head and shouts, "How, how will you pay me for my son? How?"

And again the wind taps on the windows in Majdanek: Remember the devil's ovens, Pole, remember the camp of death! Remember the millions of tortured, shot, burned! Remember and take revenge!

On the square in front of Lublin Castle huge crowds have gathered to pay homage over the ashes of the martyrs.

A choir sings the ancient "Bogarodzica," the prayer with which the Polish army went out to fight the Germans in the fields of Grunwald.

The crowd sobs… Little girls in white skirts put wreaths on the graves. Women in black, widows of victims, sink to the ground.

Soldiers of the Polish Army stand with heads bared. Soldiers of the Red Army present arms.

A solemn mass is conducted by the Rev. Dr. Kruszyński. Over the ashes of the martyrs he calls their relatives to unite. W. Rzymowski, member of the Polish Committee for National Liberation, places a memorial plaque on the wall of Lublin Castle. The Short inscription reads:

> "To the million victims murdered by the German criminals in Majdanek and in Lublin Castle. August 6, 1944. The Polish People."

Former prisoners bear an urn containing ashes from the Majdanek crematorium. The urn is placed in the castle wall. A delegation from the Red Army lays a wreath from the army and the people of the USSR. Twenty-five thousand people gathered on the square sing an old anti-German song. The words have the ring of an oath:

> *No more will the German spit in our face,*
> *Nor Germanize our children.*

From the blood of the victims, in the fire of war, in fraternal unity with the Soviet people, a new, free Poland rises from the ashes.

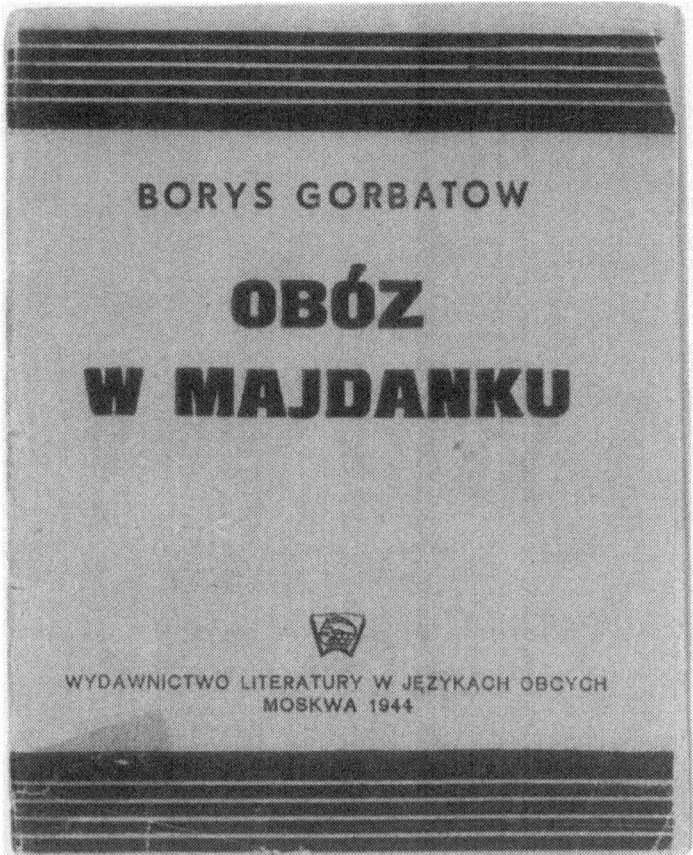

BORYS GORBATOW

OBÓZ
W MAJDANKU

WYDAWNICTWO LITERATURY W JĘZYKACH OBCYCH
MOSKWA 1944

Photographs found among papers of victims in the extermination camp.

Extermination camp at Lublin. Entire camp was surrounded by double rows of barbed wire fence, continuously charged with high-voltage electricity.

Shoes of death camp victims.

Canisters of "Zyklon," lethal gas employed by Germans to asphyxiate their victims.

www.ingramcontent.com/pod-product-compliance
Lightning Source LLC
Chambersburg PA
CBHW030309290526
45785CB00001B/274